A LIFE IN FULL

MILLICENT ROGERS

4/17/2015
At Monty's house

For Monty,

From 4th grade To graduation from
Southeastern Lab School. Such a sweet
special Southern girl who never got
in Trouble & doesn't remember The
night we were cruizing for a bruising
& the back seat on my Jigger caught
on fire. Love you Montjoy,
Your Nita
Murphy

A LIFE IN FULL

MILLICENT ROGERS

BY ARTHUR J. BACHRACH, NITA MURPHY, AND JUDITH NASSE

COVER PHOTOGRAPH - TAOS GORGE BY GERAINT SMITH

ADDITIONAL PHOTOGRAPHY BY DAVE CORDOVA

Cover and interior design: Lesley Cox

FEEL Design Associates, Taos, New Mexico

Cover photo: Geraint Smith, Rio Grande Gorge Overlook

(Courtesy Geraint Smith Photography.)

Millicent in a cameo of one of her Navajo pieces.

(Photos courtesy Millicent Rogers Museum.)

www.abqpress.com

Albuquerque, New Mexico

www.abqpress.com

978-0-9838712-7-9

DEDICATION

Art Bachrach, 1923–2011, is deeply missed. We are sad that he won't be able to see this book published and on the shelves as he would have enjoyed the book signings with his usual heartiness of wit and deep interest in all the people and the events around him. This book about Millicent Rogers is a result of Art's inspiration and friendship with Paul Peralta-Ramos, Millicent's youngest son. Art was a raconteur, a scholar, and a gentleman whose deep curiosity led him to explore the lives of Taoseños and then translate them into words, either through his books or his stories told to friends. He and Millicent shared a love of the world's literature, collecting fascinating libraries, both speaking other languages, and both spending many hours reading and sharing their love of what they read.

— NM and JN

Photo of Art Bachrach (Courtesy Nita Murphy.)

MILLICENT ROGERS

ACKNOWLEDGMENTS

This book would not have been possible without the co-operation and marvelous reminiscences of Arturo Peralta-Ramos, the last surviving son of Millicent Rogers. Jackie Peralta-Ramos, Arturo's wife, has also contributed stories and generously opened her home for research. Millicent's son Paul's children, Phillip Peralta-Ramos and Christina Lucia Peralta-Ramos Luera, have provided support, as has Antonia Salm, Peter's daughter. Wiltraud Salm, widow of Peter Salm, Millicent's oldest son, provided additional material, especially about the Salm family history.

We deeply appreciate Susan Bachrach, Art's wife; Eric Lambert, Nita's friend; and Book Writing World and KWB, Judith's friends, for their unwavering support.

To Judith Van Gieson of ABQ Press, our friend, editor, and publisher. We are deeply indebted to her for helping us through the sea of publishing and for her encouragement to keep going for Art's sake.

Linda Triegel's help in the final copy editing proved invaluable. We also appreciate Lesley Cox, of

Feel Design Associates, Taos, for her superb work on the book design.

The staff at the Millicent Rogers Museum, including Executive Director Fred Peralta, Carmela Duran, and Joy Jensen, were extremely helpful in providing encouragement and in giving access to the Millicent Rogers archives.

Miranda Levy, a friend of Millicent's, generously shared her memories of Millicent Rogers visiting her store, The Thunderbird in Santa Fe, where Millicent bought jewelry, frequently accompanied by Janet Gaynor and Claudette Colbert, Hollywood friends. Others who generously shared stories with us include Tony Reyna, Julian Robles, Peter Schaeffer, Bill Green, Patricia Concha Murphy, Mark Romero, Carmen Velarde, Kurt Von Schuschnigg, Jr., and Rosmarie Matt from Haus Rudi Matt in St. Anton, Austria.

Debbie Charpentier from the Millicent Library in Fairhaven, Massachusetts, gave us valuable information and photos regarding Millicent's childhood home. David Farmer lent his excellent support and encouragement. Jeri Glover worked in the initial programming of the manuscript. David Cooper's diligent research on Millicent's Delage and her World War II activities has enriched this book. The Naval Historical Foundation sent us information about Claremont when it was a rehabilitation center for naval aviators.

The Harry Ransom Center, University of Texas at Austin, provided the letters from Millicent Rogers to the Honorable Dorothy Brett. Chris Dean provided the Ian Fleming photo from the cover of Life magazine. Rick Romancito and R. C. Israel kindly lent us photos.

FOREWORD

Millicent Rogers, MR to the three of us, was not the usual "mother" as most people would characterize the word. Not because she didn't want to be, rather in numerous ways she could not be, for life did not give her that fulfilling a luxury. She was a tigress with three cubs. Yet to the outside world much was wrongly misinterpreted as apathy. MR gave each of us independence to think and live life the way we felt and envisioned it. If and when we appeared to be going in an inappropriate direction, unknowingly to our minds or propensity, she would once again point us in the right direction and make us feel we had come to that resolution on our own. We each saw, respected, and loved her in dissimilar ways, yet related to her in respectful, diversely multifarious ways. It was not till after she died that we, in various conversations, realized she had respected, treated, and loved us in unequivocally different ways, to suit our individual personalities.

In her way she lived intensely and passionately on the edge and within each day, always aware there might not be another day for her, yet never allowing pity to rule her life within herself or to permit others, including we three, to be aware of her fragility.

She abhorred publicity or any form of notoriety. Though flaunting social convention, she was extremely private regarding matters she considered important, such as family affairs. She was fiercely loyal to her friends, copiously philanthropic and a fervent anti-Nazi activist during World War II. She fought social injustices for the Southwest Native Americans.

She was artistically gifted, with a remarkable sense of design, was passionate with multiple husbands and lovers, highly intelligent, socially prominent, well dressed, flamboyant and original, with a lively sense of humor, profusely extravagant, and in many ways extremely truthful and blunt. However, she was vehemently secretive in much of what she did or accomplished in her life. Because of this, much misinformation surrounded her in all forms of the media and especially in articles constantly being inaccurately written about her through made-up false hypothetical assumptions. From the time she was a young girl, she was constantly referred to as the "Standard Oil Heiress," which upset her significantly throughout her life. That most probably led her to being so secretive.

Over the years after MR's death, both Paul and I were approached numerous times by individuals wanting to write stories or a biography about her. Since both of us knew and saw MR in totally different aspects, we always conferred and rejected their request. After Paul's demise, numerous requests continued and were as usual rejected. From pressure by Paul's and my children and grandchildren to allow the intimate history of the family to be written by the last remaining member of the family, I finally acquiesced with apprehension and quite some uncertainty.

After much time and many hours of conference with one of Paul's best friends, Art Bachrach, the story began. First with letters, old news and magazine articles, forgotten pictures, and the probing of my recollection of long-forgotten instances of time and memory, a story began to unfold that even I found hard to fathom and believe of my mother's past. The story includes high fashion, skiing and bobsledding, sex, cars, spies, multiple international husbands and lovers, family, and close friends. She was a unique eyewitness and apparently hidden participant in some of the most important events of the twentieth century. Beset by serious health issues from an early age, she believed each day could be her last. As was once expressed, "Burning hotly, illuminating the shadows, she lived a life in full until the flame burnt out."

Without the help of numerous individuals who never even knew her, like David Cooper who became so intrigued with her life that he became immensely helpful to me in researching this story. He helped to uncover much of her concealed past from looking at the accumulated names of her civilian, political, and military friends. I connected these people to her and gradually uncovered the prior unsuspected secret part of her life in WWII.

I acknowledge the patient hours that Nita Murphy and Judith Nasse spent gently tapping and jolting my past memory of times, names, and instances that I had thought were long forgotten. But most of all I praise Art

Bachrach, who became as interested and fascinated as I had become in finding all these new unknown facets of my mother's life.

— ARTURO PERALTA-RAMOS II, MARCH 15, 2010

TABLE OF CONTENTS

PROLOGUE

— The Rio Grande —

"Why hasn't anyone ever told me about this place?" Millicent Rogers asked Janet Gaynor as they stood at the edge of the Rio Grande Gorge near Taos, New Mexico, on August 15, 1947.

Rick Romancito, "Rio Grande Gorge." (Courtesy Rick Romancito.)

Actress and friend Gaynor brought Millicent to Taos following Millicent's tumultuous breakup with Clark Gable after a year's affair in Hollywood. Gaynor and her husband, Gilbert Adrian, the Hollywood costume designer, were familiar with Taos, having visited often.

Millicent was enchanted with the beauty of the place. Seven hundred feet below her the Rio Grande River, with its headwaters in Colorado, flowed swiftly. Taos, at an altitude of 7,000 feet, is surrounded by the Sangre de Cristo Mountain Range. *Sangre de Cristo* ("Blood of Christ") was so named by the Spanish Conquistadors in the sixteenth century as they viewed the brilliant red sunsets reflected on the range.

After living in many places on three continents, Millicent remained in Taos until her untimely death in 1953.

Millicent Rogers: born into great opulence - buried in an Indian blanket.

— JACQUELINE PARALTA-RAMOS

EARLY HISTORY

O n the evening of November 19, 1919, 2,000 invited guests at the New York Ritz-Carlton Hotel awaited the appearance of Millicent Rogers. Millicent, the daughter of Colonel and Mrs. Henry Huddleston[1] Rogers and granddaughter of Standard Oil tycoon Henry Huttleson Rogers, Sr., wore brocaded and plain white satin with lace panniers and a tiny green wreath at the side of her frock, with another wreath in her blonde hair. According to the November 25, 1919, *New York Times* account of the event, "Millicent greeted her guests from the top of one of the wide stairways" in the Crystal Room. It was probably the largest ball of the season.

The ballroom's autumn décor was lavishly filled with tall oak trees with russet foliage, umbrella shaped trees topped with chrysanthemums, pots of varied colored chrysanthemums, and Australian tree ferns tied with centerpieces of green orchids. Guests danced to a thirty-piece orchestra throughout the evening. Among the guests were members of the British, Italian, and French Diplomatic Corps in Washington and New York Society.

Arturo Peralta-Ramos II says of his mother's demeanor, "As a person she was probably nowhere near beautiful, but when she walked into a room, she had a stunning presence. She walked with the grace of a swan, and with her slow, soft voice; and she was glamorous. She knew make-up expertly."[2]

This beautiful debutante's life began on February 2, 1902, in New York. Her given name was Mary Abigail Millicent Rogers.

Millicent Rogers and the Colonel, 1904. (Courtesy Peralta-Ramos Family Archives.)

She was raised in Manhattan and on the lavish 1,200-acre Southampton estate with a Tuscan inspired home known as The Beach House, with gardens by internationally acclaimed landscape architect Frederick

Law Olmsted, who also designed Central Park in New York. The estate contained the hunting lodge, Port of Missing Men, on the North Shore of Long Island. The name "Port of Missing Men" came from the shipwreck of 1893 on the local coast. *Lycanes Valley* and its tug *Panther* went down with 17 men. The Colonel later found a rudder from the wreck on his Wald IV beach property at Southampton.

"The Port of Missing Men, with its roughly 2,000-acre wild, wooded peninsula known as Cow Neck, became H.H. Rogers' wild duck shooting ground, wherein he had five major shooting lakes dredged from marsh swamps. On the boundaries of the lakes, and on the islands, he placed two-man metal buried shooting blinds, so that he and his guests did not get cold while waiting for the ducks to fly into the lakes. The blinds had heaters built into them as well as telephone communications to the building on the mainland of the property."[3]

In 1905, when she was three years old, Millicent's brother, Henry Rogers III. was born. In a letter to Mark Twain, Henry said, about the young Henry's baptism, "Millicent ran through the house telling the guests that Henry was to be 'atomized' on Sunday."[4]

As a small child, she played in Central Park and wore her hair braided in large macaroons over her ears. As well as Southampton, she grew up on large rented estates and in rented castles in Scotland. Her early schooling was at Miss Maderia's School in Virginia and with private tutors. At the age of eight she had a serious bout of rheumatic fever that plagued her health for the rest of her life. Often bedridden, she taught herself French, German, Italian and Greek, and fluent Latin.

With her knowledge of German, she translated the work of the poet Rilke.

Her son Arturo said of his mother, "(She) lived in and through her own imagination because of her illness and her inability to play with other children."

Millicent and her brother Henry. (Courtesy Peralta-Ramos Family archives.)

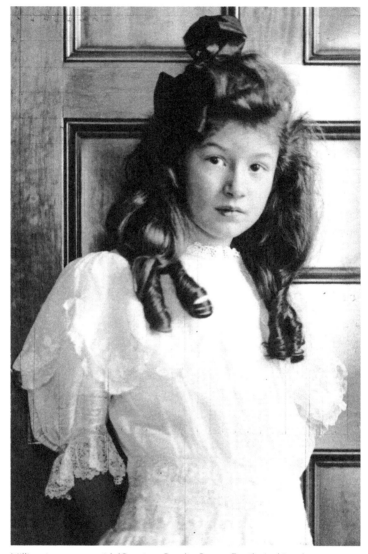

Millicent as a young girl. (Courtesy Peralta-Ramos Family Archives.)

Arturo observed in Shelby Tisdale's book, *Fine Indian Jewelry of the Southwest: The Millicent Rogers Museum Collection*, "She was separated from her childhood peers by this lingering lifetime and intimidating illness. In a way she learned to live life within herself because of not being capable of sharing childhood experiences with others. Her playmates and conceptions were elicited and envisioned from perceived fathoms within her own imaginative mind. She grew up realizing she could never do and be like others. To occupy her time she studied art in all its beautiful creative and assorted forms."[5]

Dave Cordova. Copy of Millicent's diary page 52. "Millicent reading in bed." (Courtesy Arturo Peralta-Ramos II.)

Arturo relates, "One Sunday Henry Rogers Senior announced to the family, 'There will be a man who will be joining us for dinner who has a different color of skin than us. This man is very important and will go down in history one day. Anybody who is not comfortable with this may leave.' Everyone showed up." Arturo added that his mother was surprised by the first black man she had ever seen. Millicent may have been about seven years old. The guest was Booker T. Washington, who was also the first black man to dine at the White House.

As Millicent grew older, her life became filled with social functions in Southampton. She loved camping when her health allowed such activity. Dogs and other animals were always a part of her life.

In her personal diary of 1917-18, which she copied from her original diary because, as Millicent wrote, "Mother has taken to reading it," (the first 34 pages had been torn out) she wrote of activities that were typical of the era for a 15-year-old in her social setting. These included singing in the church choir and being confirmed on March 25th at St James Church, when "the whole damn family was there!" She was editor of her school magazine, acted in a school play, took drawing and painting lessons, and went to dentist appointments and countless teas, horse shows, and motoring trips from New York to the Southampton estate. Included in the diary was a hand-drawn map of Tuxedo Park, her grandmother's home, where she attended a benefit for the Red Cross. She wrote of enjoying a course in home nursing and first aid and learning to knit and crochet. She mentions wondering why she got a cold every two weeks. It is interesting that it is the only reference to her health in her diary.[6]

In April of that year, she commented in her diary, "Ma & Pa gone south…where do I come in I wonder?" Then, in the only entry for November, Millicent writes, "Kicked off to boarding school."

Atypical of her age were the depth of comments which revealed her sensibilities of World War I. "War is all everyone speaks of. The Bosh[7] – we'll show them. Death and orphaned children. War has been declared. Thank God. Now we can help give them hell. It will mean death. Dead everywhere."

Her mother took Millicent to London as a teenager where members of British society welcomed her as a young, charming American princess.[8] Attending

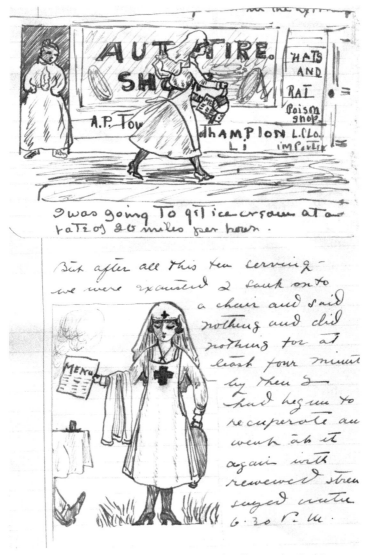

Dave Cordova. Copy of Millicent's diary page with Millicent in her Red Cross Uniform. (Courtesy Arturo Peralta-Ramos II)

many social events in New York and Europe, she characteristically wore stunning and outrageous gowns. She also traveled to China and France with her parents, returning to America in 1918, where the family had a home at 1624 K Street in Washington, D.C. In 1919 she wore a sensational Chinese headdress and Mandarin robe, that she brought back from China, at one of the many society balls she attended. Beginning in 1920 Millicent was on both the American and the World's "Best Dressed List" for most of her life.

If she is remembered for nothing else, it would be Millicent's astonishingly original personal style and design, which permeated everything she did, from her presentation and appearance, to her houses, her extensive collections of art and jewelry, her custom Delage automobile, her parties, even her affairs and marriages. In essence, Millicent's whole life was her own original composition. Millicent's design sense was partly self-tutored during the many hours she was confined to bed, studying art and design. From her family, she was exposed to many cultural and visual experiences in their travels, and she was surrounded by art and design through her parents' many varied friends.

Though she worked with Charles James periodically, she also made designs, worked with, and was friends with Elsa Schiaparelli, Coco Chanel, and the Fabergé collection. "Millicent was often dressed by the leading couturiers of her day—Schiaparelli, Mainbocher, and Valentina. She had the unique ability to get designers to make clothes for her exactly as she wanted them. It was that talent that allowed her to go beyond the current fashions to create her own style."[9]

Among her many admirers, she was courted by the Prince of Wales on his American tour and Serge Obolensky, the exiled white Russian Prince and Czarist colonel. Obolensky later became one of the first members

Millicent in 1918 or 1919. (Courtesy Peralta-Ramos Family archives.)

of the newly constructed U.S. intelligence service, the Office of Strategic Services, organized by General William Donovan. Obolensky recalled, "Millicent was terribly attractive, one of the most beautiful girls I have ever known. She was an exotic creature, with a curious languid manner. Even her voice, soft and pensive, was that of an Oriental, and she generally dressed the part."[10] After the affair ended, Obolensky remained a friend.

1920 brought her engagement to Mr. James Thompson of New York. Apparently disapproving of her engagement, her mother whisked her off to Europe again, and while she was abroad, her engagement to Thompson was broken by mutual consent. When she was in England, the *Fort Worth Star-Telegram* wrote, "Rumors floated back that she was betrothed to a British peer. But, if she was, she must have jilted him too. Because she is back in the States now and Mr. Thompson once more is fluttering around and about."[11]

Millicent and her parents were back in Europe in 1921 enjoying the social circle in London. An article in the July 1921 *Ogden Standard Examiner* stated, "King George and Queen Mary today gave a garden party at Buckingham Palace to some 4,000 guests. Included among Americans present were Colonel E.M. House and Mrs. House, Colonel H.H. Rogers, Mrs. Rogers and Miss Millicent Rogers, Archibald Roosevelt…. The gowns worn by the women were rather more subdued than those seen at Ascot and the Henley regatta. Most of the skirts were longer than those lately considered fashionable."[12]

While in Europe this time, Millicent fell in love with the Duke d'Aosta of Italy, who proposed marriage, but the Colonel (her father) would not give his consent. Her father's opposition was matched by Mussolini's rule forbidding marriage to a member of the House of Savoy by a foreigner. "It was Count Galeazzo Ciano, son-in-law of Mussolini, who gave the order forbidding Mother to marry," recounts Arturo Peralta-Ramos. Miffed, Millicent told her father that she would marry the next man who proposed to her.

On March 1, 1922, the Colonel sent Millicent a letter regarding her expenditures (the spelling and punctuation are the Colonel's):

My dear Millicent: -

Miss Watson handed me to-day your account with the office and on analyzing it I am extremely annoyed because you do not seem to appreciate the value of money nor to realize that there is an obligation on your part to keep your expenditures within the limit of your allowance.

You will recall that last year in France I increased your allowance and paid your bills and it was distinctly understood by you that from that time until the first of June you only had a credit of $1,000. If you look over the attached list you will see that since our return here you have spent $1,871.88 on bills which I have paid at the office, and in addition to this by mistake Miss Watson sent out a check on the first of January 1922 for $333.33, so that since our return to New York your total expenditures have been $1,871.88, in other words you have spent $871.88 more than your allowance up to the first of June.

You are now twenty years old and presumeably should have arrived at a mental condition in which you could perform the simple mathematical problems of addition and subtraction, and to have known quite distinctly that you had spent more money than you had. I cannot imagine, under the circumstances, a more idiotic thing for any one to do, having just arrived from Paris and having bought quantities of clothes to immediately rush off and buy a Red Crepe Beaded Gown for $250.00, when you only had $1,000. to carry you over until the first of June, and under these conditions you run up a bill of $457.50 at Cartiers, the most expensive place in New York, when if any of these were necessary, by going to a smaller and cheaper jeweler, you could have gotten the same return for less money.

I call this matter to your attention now as I do not want you to make any more purchases of clothes, etc. abroad until my arrival, when I will discuss this matter with you.

You will note by the foregoing that no more money is due you on your allowance until the middle of August, and I expect hereafter that you will show a reasonable amount of common sense in your expenditures.

Affectionately,

Fairhaven, 1905 or 1906. (Courtesy Peralta-Ramos Family archives.)

THE ROGERS FAMILY

illicent Rogers came from a socially prominent philanthropic, and intellectually stimulating family.

The story of Henry Huttleston Rogers, Millicent's grandfather, is characteristic of the American Dream. A young man from humble beginnings, who through hard work and enterprise, achieved a life of wealth and social standing, Henry became one of the most prominent men in America. He was born in 1840, the son of Roland and Mary Huttleston Rogers. The Rogers were of early New England ancestry and descended from Mayflower stock. A maternal grandfather was a successful shipmaster and three of Henry's great-grandfathers fought in the Revolutionary War.

Henry grew up in Fairhaven, Massachusetts, where he delivered newspapers and worked as a clerk and grocery delivery boy for five years after high school graduation. In 1861 he became a brakeman and baggage man on the Fairhaven Branch Railroad where he developed his love of railroads. Starting in the oil field in Pennsylvania, he and a friend built a small refinery. They made a profit of $30,000 the first year, approximately $700,000 today. This venture began his entry into high finance.

Henry returned to Fairhaven in 1862 and married Abigail Palmer Gifford, his high school sweetheart. They had six children. One son died in infancy, and a daughter, Millicent Gifford, died in 1890, at the age of 17, of a heart ailment. Millicent Gifford had a passionate love of books, and the family built the beautiful library in her name which is still operating in Fairhaven. The other children were Cara, Mai, Anne, and Henry II.

H. H. Rogers with grandchildren. Millicent is standing on his left.
(Courtesy Peralta-Ramos Family archives.)

Henry's wife, Abigail, died following surgery in 1894. Henry then married Emilie Augusta Randel Hart. No children came from this union. Henry died in 1909 and Emilie in 1912.

Henry Rogers' wealth, estimated at up to $350 million upon his death, was a long step from his father Roland's income. Roland earned the sum of $95.20 in three years as a member of the crew on a whaling ship, the 147th share of the catch. By age 53, Henry was one of the leaders of the Standard Oil Trust, of which there were 20 companies. He was the president of six and the director of thirteen. Having amassed a fortune, Rogers was typical of the oil and railroad barons of the era in his philanthropic works. Publically he was sometimes known as the "Hell Hound of Wall Street" for his sharp, determined, and ruthless business practices.

Henry insisted on keeping all his philanthropy confidential, just as his granddaughter Millicent would do years later. He was a benefactor of Booker T. Washington, Helen Keller and, most well known, Samuel Clemens, better known as Mark Twain, whom he rescued from bankruptcy. Mark Twain was in dire financial straits owing to a disastrous investment in his own publishing house. Rogers, a deep admirer of Twain, advanced funds to bail him out, placed the Clemens' New England home in Libby Clemens' name to prevent foreclosure, and straightened out their finances. Twain embarked on a yearlong lecture tour to earn enough money to repay Rogers. They became close, lifelong friends.

Another bond between Rogers and Twain was their mutual loss of a beloved daughter at a young age, Rogers daughter Millicent Gifford at 17 and Twain's daughter Suzy at 24. Rogers and Twain spent a lot of time on the yacht *Kanawha*, which won the 1903 and 1904 Lysistrata Cup doing 20 knots. "...the *Kanawha's* funnel left a pale brown trace behind, the result of her hand-picked coal. It was no small consideration that *Kanawha* was owned by Henry Huttleston Rogers...who also happened to own the Virginian Railway...which just happened to haul coal from the Kanawha mines."[13]

The senior Rogers carried on an extensive correspondence with Mark Twain, and Twain continued to write to Mary Benjamin Rogers, Millicent's mother, until his death in 1910. Millicent's sons, Peter L. Salm and Arturo Peralta-Ramos, presented these letters to Columbia University in 1953, and *Letters to Mary* was published in 1961. Twain dedicated his book, *Following the Equator,* "to Harry," Millicent's father.

Henry and Mark Twain aboard the Kanawha: from left to right:
Augustus G. Paine (New York business man), Henry H. Rogers, Thomas B Reed
(a former Speaker of the House), Mark Twain, Laurence Hutton (an editor
at Harper's Magazine and a lecturer at Princeton), W. T. Foote (lawyer and
congressman), and Clarence C. Rice (doctor who introduced Rogers and Twain).
(Courtesy Millicent Library, Fairhaven, MA.)

On August 14, 1906, Twain wrote to Mary Rogers, "Ho, you miraculous combination of quick- silver, watch springs and sunshine, how you do dance out from your pen and light up this solemn solitude and set things a moving! No matter how long you live you'll never get old, (thanks be!). My wife never did, neither did my mother: and my mother lived to be 88, and always she was all animation and champagne and charm, like you!"[14]

The senior Rogers, according to the Booker T. Washington papers,[15] donated large sums of money, usually in cash, to Tuskegee Institute and at least 65 other Southern schools. He built a 600 mile railroad in the coal mining region of Virginia, and into his West Virginia Kanawha coal mines. He expressed concern about the welfare of the people living alongside it. Washington wrote, "He arranged for me to make a trip over his new Virginia railway for the purpose of studying the condition of the colored people along the route and of devising some means by which he might assist them in their education and in the development of their agricultural life." Working with Washington, Henry quietly funded the 65 small country schools along the route for the education and betterment of African-Americans. A station along the route was named Huttleston in his honor. Rogers and Washington were close friends over a 15-year period. It was only after Rogers' death that Washington felt free to reveal the identity of his generous benefactor.

Mark Twain spoke to Rogers about a bright young woman, who was severely handicapped, named Helen Keller. Rogers was touched by the determination of this young woman and paid her expenses to Radcliffe College. He provided a monthly stipend to support her for the rest of her life. Her first autobiography, *The Story of My Life*, credits Henry Huttleston Rogers with his generosity and also notes his desire to have such beneficence kept secret.

Millicent's father, Colonel Henry Huddleston Rogers, was a student of American military history. Also known as Harry, he was commander of a field artillery unit in World War I and saw action in the French Offensive for which he received both the U.S. Distinguished Service Medal and the French Croix de Guerre. His hobby was collecting naval sailing-ship models and whaling ships in particular. His extensive collection of ship models, dating from 1650 to 1830, was given to the U.S. Naval Academy in Annapolis. The class of 1952 donated the funds for a building to house this exceptional collection. It is now open to the public. A second collection of whaling-ship models, along with their original log books, was donated to Mystic Seaport in New London, Connecticut. Later, Millicent's son Paul was a director of Mystic Seaport for many years.

Harry was the vice president and general manager of the Atlantic Coast Railroad and took over his father's seat on the board of the Virginian Railway.

Millicent's Aunt Cara married a British citizen, Urban Hanlon Broughton, a Member of Parliament. She became Lady Fairhaven. It was common practice in Britain, when someone was granted the title, for the honored person to choose a name with which he or she was associated. An example is of the British Field Marshall, Bernard Law Montgomery, who, when honored, became Viscount Montgomery of Alamein, the North African site of his major victory. When Cara was granted the title, she chose the name Fairhaven, the beloved family home in Massachusetts. This was the first time in British history that an American site was used in a title. In 1915 she gave the British Crown a 182.5-

acre meadow at Runnymede, which she had purchased to save from becoming a housing development. It is the historic site of the signing of the Magna Carta. It was for this generosity that Queen Victoria gave her the title in perpetuity.

Mary Benjamin Rogers, Millicent's mother, also came from a distinguished family. Her father, George Hillard Benjamin, held multiple academic degrees. He was a practicing physician, patent expert, and industrial engineer. He was also skilled as a criminologist, applying his wide knowledge of chemistry to solving crimes. Mary Benjamin was well known by the Rogers family. Mary's uncle, William Evarts Benjamin, was married to Henry Huttleston's daughter Anne. William Evarts Benjamin, along with Millicent's grandfather, had helped Mark Twain during his financial troubles by purchasing the Library of American Literature, Twain's failed publishing venture. Mary Benjamin's grandfather, Park Benjamin, was a poet and journalist in New York and an associate of Horace Greeley in founding *The New York Tribune.*

Mary Benjamin and Harry were married in 1900. At the time Twain sent Mary a letter of congratulations and well wishes. Harry and Mary spent a year abroad, and, in 1902, their first child, Millicent, was born. In 1905, Henry H. Rogers III was born.

After Millicent's parents divorced in 1929, her father married three more times-to Virginia Lincoln, Daisy Fields, and his eventual widow, Pauline Hoving.

Millicent's mother, after her divorce, had a long relationship with Bernard Boutet de Monvel, a renowned French artist. Boutet encouraged Mary Benjamin Rogers to paint, and she had a studio in Boutet's building in

Paris. The late Peter Salm once said, "Bernard taught her to paint, persuaded her to paint...." She painted until her death in 1957. Boutet painted a portrait of Millicent, in 1948, "angular beauty, emerging from the silken meringue of a Charles James gown...."

Bernard Boutet de Monvel, Portrait of Mary Benjamin Rogers, 1930. (Courtesy Arturo Peralta-Ramos II.)

The family home in Fairhaven was another example of the culmination of the success of the Rogers family. It was an 85-room mansion, each family member having his or her own wing. There were 18 bedrooms, children's play rooms, bowling alleys, a wine cellar, kitchens large enough for a deluxe hotel, cold storage, and its own gas plant. After the death of his stepmother, Harry, recognizing that the mansion was not being used, decided that the cost of maintaining it gave no reason

Bernard Boutet de Monvel, Portrait of Millicent Rogers, 1948.
(Courtesy Arturo Peralta-Ramos II.)

to continue its support. Harry offered the mansion to the town of Fairhaven, who turned it down. In 1915 the mansion was turned over to wreckers. The foreman of the wrecking crew, Mr. Donnelly, told a reporter, "A fellow grows unsentimental in this business but it seemed almost a sacrilege to tear down this magnificent memory of Mr. Rogers, whose hand you can see in every elaborate detail." The residents of Fairhaven, who watched Henry grow from a grocery clerk to an oil baron, realized that a glamorous era in their town had come to an end.

Fairhaven. (Courtesy Peralta-Ramos Family archives.)

Standing on the Fairhaven grounds were two 50-foot-tall copper beech trees. Before the demolition could damage them, Mai Rogers Coe, Millicent's aunt, who had played under these trees as a child, had the trees, with their massive root balls and weighing 38 tons each, moved a distance of 300 miles by water to Oyster Bay, Long Island, at a cost of $4,000 in December of 1914. This took 12 working days and a team of 72 horses, plus ships, to help in the transplanting. One of these trees survives to this day.

Henry Rogers III, Millicent's brother, was educated at Oxford University in England. Arturo Peralta-Ramos states, "Sadly for Henry his father, the Colonel as he was referred to by all, always put him mentally down, even as a child. No matter what he did, he could do nothing right in the Colonel's eyes! Though his mother, MBR, as all mothers would, defended his weaknesses, especially that of not being a strong athletic' individual. In the eyes of today he would have been considered a 'nerd' and a 'weakling,' whose only interest was in books of modern science and ancient scientific history."[16]

Henry III married Virginia Lincoln from Ohio in 1929. Later he was implicated in the death of actress Evelyn Hoey, who died of a gunshot wound to her head, during a party, in his home in Pennsylvania on September 11, 1935. Her death was officially declared a suicide. Henry III was soon cut out of his father's will owing to his errant behavior.

Henry married a dancer, Diana Taylor, in May of 1937. In 1948 he died in California at age 43 of cirrhosis of the liver. According to Arturo, Henry was good with his hands and mind. In 1942 Henry declared to Arturo, "I would rather cast a generator part than anything else I can think of." Arturo adds, "As adults Millicent and her brother did have a close relationship. My uncle was always put down by his father. Uncle Henry created and patented many inventions in his lifetime." From childhood, Millicent and Henry talked to each other in Latin when they wished to have a private discussion.

Mary Benjamin Rogers met Van Day Truex, father of twentieth-century design and later president of the Parsons School of Design, through her friend and lover, teacher, and portrait painter Bernard Boutet de Monvel. Adam Lewis in his book about Truex writes, "From the moment Mary Rogers met Truex, she unabashedly loved him as a surrogate son. H.H. Rogers III, her natural son, had always been a sad disappointment to her, beset as he was by a serious drinking problem and a life of scandal that had virtually alienated him from both of his parents. Truex was Mary Rogers' ideal. Her grandson, Paul Peralta-Ramos, remembers, 'Van was all that she had wanted her son to be. In her mind he was perfect. Van was so much a part of our life that he even called my brother Arturo, "Brother." This pet name was reserved only for members of our family.' Millicent, too, was captivated by Truex. As her older son, Arturo Peralta-Ramos, recalls, 'By the time our mother and father were married in 1927, and certainly before I was born in 1928 and Paul in 1931, Van was already accepted as one of the family. He and mother had a unique friendship. She was devoted to him.' Realizing that Truex had little money, Mary and Millicent both made sure that he never wanted for anything. Neither of them saw this as charity; for Mary Rogers, giving money to Truex was the same as taking care of her own children."[17]

"In his best form, Truex entertained Mary Rogers and her family with witty conversation … Over the years, he had become so much a part of the family, and was so often with their grandmother, that the young Peralta-Ramos boys thought he was a relative; they could not remember a Christmas or family celebration that had not included him."[18]

Millicent Rogers and Jane Fonda were second cousins on Mary Benjamin Rogers' side. In her autobiography, *My Life So Far*, Jane describes the relationship of her mother, Frances Ford Seymour. to the Rogers, "Grandfather's sister, Jane Seymour Benjamin, had a daughter, Mary, who was married to Colonel H.H. Rogers, a professional military man and the son and heir of Henry Huttleston Rogers…."[19] Fonda goes on to say that life on her grandmother's farm in Canada was hard, so "Mary (Benjamin Rogers) decided to bring her cousins to Fairhaven, Massachusetts.

"Mother spent the two final years of high school in Fairhaven and was doted on by her cousin Mary and Mary's daughter Millicent Rogers, six years my mother's senior. Millicent was to become a strikingly beautiful and fashionable socialite, jewelry designer, and humanitarian. The Millicent Rogers Museum in Taos, New Mexico, which houses part of her art collection and the heavy gold and silver jewelry she designed, is testimony to her talent and taste. These relatives of Mother's were interesting, gracious, strong women–the glue that held things together–and they must have been powerful role models. But Mother makes clear in the history she wrote that she was shy and intimidated by them. In her medical records, her doctor wrote, 'Always she felt painfully inadequate and inferior socially and intellectually as the poor cousin.'"[20]

Millicent and her 3 husbands: from left to right:
Count Ludwig Salm van Hoogstraeten, Arturo Peralta-Ramos I,
and Ronald Balcom.
(Courtesy Albuquerque Journal, April 3, 1938.)

MILLICENT'S MARRIAGES AND SONS

illicent followed her prophecy to her father that she would marry the first man she met after her father rejected the proposal from Duke d'Aosta. Millicent's flamboyant history of marriages and affairs began in 1924 when she married her first husband, Count Ludwig Salm van Hoogstraeten, 17 years her senior. The count was physically attractive, a Davis Cup tennis player, a former WWI Austrian officer, a cavalryman, and a playboy. He was born in Bad Homburg, Germany, on February 24, 1885. The Salm family originally had extensive holdings from Germany into Belgium awarded to them by Charlemagne in the 900's AD. The holdings, to the west of the Rhine, were confiscated by Napoleon, and the Schloss in Belgium is now a military institution. The Count's branch of the family, though without any extensive properties, still holds the highest title of "Graf" (German for Count). The Count published a book in 1929, *Mein Lieber Peter, Beichte eines Vaters* (*My Dear Peter, Confessions of a Father*), documenting his family's history.

One of the illustrious ancestors of the Count was Graf Nicolas zu Salm-Reifferscheidt, who played a prominent role in the Battle of Vienna in 1529 at the age of 70. Graf Nicholas was too minor a noble to be named as a commander, yet his decisions to shore up the walls of Vienna and to prepare the city for the siege by Sultan Sulieman of Constantinople proved to be decisive in the winning of the battle. By the night of October 12, 1529, the Ottoman army struck its tents.

"Graf Salm was hit in the hip by the splinters of a stone ball during the attack, a wound from which he never recovered, but Vienna was kept awake by the light of fires, as the Janissaries burned everything not portable, and by the screams as they threw their prisoners into the fire. Next morning they were gone. It snowed.

Statue of Graf Nicholas Salm in Vienna.
(Courtesy Austrian Embassy.)

"In the deserted camps the Austrians found some curious-looking brown beans. They boiled them; the beans themselves were not very good, but the soup that came from them proved quite potable. It was the first coffee in Europe."[21]

He was nearly 39 and she was almost 22 when Count Salm and Millicent were married by a justice of the peace at City Hall, in New York City, on January 8, 1924. It was rumored that the Count was so broke that Millicent paid for the wedding ring. For their honeymoon they sailed to Paris. The Colonel did not like the "fortune hunting husband" and told Millicent that she would not get one cent if she remained married to the Count. Their marriage was short lived. They were estranged four months later when the Colonel sailed to Paris and offered Salm $250,000. Millicent, pregnant, returned with the Colonel by ship. Salm took a train to Vienna to play tennis. Their son Peter was born September 27, 1924, in New York City. On December 2, 1924, the Count arrived in New York with his mother to see his son, and her grandson, for the first time. The Count was not allowed to see his son Peter alone. Peter's nurses and specially hired guards surrounded him.

Their divorce was not final until 1927. The Count was divorced by Millicent and returned to Europe $300,000 richer.[22] Years later, in 1939, the Count sued their 14-year-old son Peter for support. Peter had received $16,000,000 in trust from his grandfather's estate in 1935.[23] *The New York Times* of April 10, 1939, states, "The Court denies the Count's plea for annual support for himself and his mother." Arturo claims this was misinformation from the press.

The Count died in mysterious circumstances. Arturo Peralta-Ramos II emphatically states, "(The Count) Peter's father did commit suicide! However, he did it out of incredible, imposing self-induced bravery! When secretly informed by the hotel desk manager, by desk phone, that the German Gestapo were on their way up to his room in Budapest and thus giving him only a matter of two, possibly three minutes, maximum before they would or could reach his floor and door. The fire exit on his floor, in the old hotel, was directly past the elevator doors. He must have instantly realized he had only two alternatives: immediate capture and tortuous interrogation or the instant horror of his own death by suicide. It appears that courageously he jumped from his window onto the glass-covered atrium below rather than be forced by torture to divulge others names he was aware of.

"Peter was terribly distressed when he learned of his father's suicide in Budapest in 1944, because he feared that his father had been a weak man and that suicide had been a coward's way out. After the war, Peter made an unsuccessful trip to find his father's burial site. To reassure my brother, I used my contacts in government and travelled to Budapest to learn the true story of the Count's death, and that it was suicide.

"Peter's father was not recognized in his life as courageous, rather was known to be extremely weak, yet his incredible hatred for the Nazis apparently made him acquiesce and become a secret courier between the approaching British Army and the Stouffenberg establishment. That group had just failed in their assassination attempt upon Hitler. He must have immediately realized he would and could not stand up their form of torture before leading to death. He indisputably knew too many names. Therefore, one must acquiesce that he died as an 'Unknown Heroic Soldier,' and not as Peter always sadly felt about his father's tragic suicide. Peter failed in his attempted search, after the war, for his father's burial site."[24]

As a child Peter was often moved around from place to place. His brother Arturo describes his screaming nightmares when he would be found clinging to his four-poster bed. Arturo, as a teasing brother, would go in and scare him. Some Christmases, when Millicent was traveling, Peter and his brothers spent the holiday with their grandmother, Mary Benjamin Rogers, wherever she was. According to Peter's widow Willi Salm, Peter never spoke of his mother or father to her.

Bernard Boutet de Monvel, Portrait of Peter Salm, 1929. It was painted in Paris at Mary Benjamin Rogers' house, 14 Rue Las Case on the Left Bank of Boulevard Saint Germain. (Courtesy Arturo Peralta-Ramos II.)

Arturo does speak fondly of his mother's attention to the boys. "She was often bedridden. She would then read to us, making up stories and drawing the illustrations for the stories. I later did that for my own children."

The naughty fapa lautic who flies around at night

Millicent Rogers, and next 3 drawings, Millcent's watercolor drawings and story. (Courtesy Millicent Rogers Museum.)

This is the grouchy Poopwineroo who has charge of all the winds when she wants the wind to change he wiggles the fan on the end of his tail. He is very disagreeable for when little boys & girls really truly want to do something tomorrow he will surely make the wind blow from the East & that make it rain if he knows they want nice weather.

The *toomiestrated* Arclightic who supplies all the lights for the jinglejungle. He has a door in the fronk of *this* tummy and all inside he's a furnace + when he wants to puh more coal on the fire he reaches down *+* with the hook on the end of his nose he opens the door latein a *crowk* full of coal + *eareeyes* which make the coal *hop* into the fire. He has two arc lights on wires that grow from the top of his head and he keeps the glasses well *dusten* with a *french* that grows on *this* head too.

"'She bounced around like mercury,' Paul Peralta-Ramos said, but adding that when he broke a leg as a child, his mother decorated his cast with a comical tale of a koala bear."[25]

"Rogers was not your everyday run-of-the-mill mother. True, she was known as the 'Standard Oil Heiress,' and to this day that invariably brings to mind big money. She was far more intelligent, interesting and comedic than one would surmise from the moniker and her youngest son, Paul Peralta-Ramos, is the first to tell you so.

"'When my brothers and I were kids we called her Mummy,' Peralta-Ramos says. 'Later, she thought Mother was too formal, and Mom didn't exactly thrill her, so we started calling her "MR" for Millicent Rogers. When we were younger, we also gave her gifts addressed to SOH. That came from the fact she was always called the Standard Oil Heiress. It was a family joke: "I'd like you to meet my mother, the Standard Oil Heiress."'[26]

"'My mother was the least judgmental person I've ever known.' Arturo Ramos (Arturo Peralta-Ramos) says. "She was totally accepting of people. She saw them as a child sees them. I always thought that was because her view of the world had been formed by books during her childhood illness. She lived with the idea of death and that fueled her incredible thirst for knowledge and total flair for living. My mother resolved that she wasn't going to die and she fought with every breath."'[27]

In her own words Millicent writes about mothering Paul to John Joseph (Paul's tutor, when she took him with her on her visit to New Mexico in 1948, see full letter on page 140), "Oh, John, I am sorry that you have decided against us; sorry for Pauliptus, for me and also for you…. I don't know what will be best for Paul …. probably to have a different kind of Mother to begin with, but since that can't be avoided, I feel that you have the freedom of thought and the individualistic concept of living life which will do him more good than all the lovely brick buildings of Americanized Georgian with the Americanized misconstruction of an English public school education. Does it really matter in what way one learns provided one does learn!

"Does one learn the difference between Hamlet and Lear more truly in a schoolroom do you think, or does one not understand better from someone who themselves feels the difference and the sadness of the two men as men; old man and young man …. will any young person ever understand the dreadful grief of age, of lost life, of unfulfilled dreams, of hope which can never be had because of life lived and past time."[28]

Growing up, Peter and Arturo attended private boarding schools in Switzerland and Germany. The two older boys learned English late returning to the US in 1939. It was their second language. They spent the summers in Venice with their grandmother. Peter prepared at Groton School. After graduation from Princeton, he worked for the State Department. Owing to his proficiency in French, Italian, German, and Spanish, he was in military intelligence, G-2, in the European theater. After the war, he went to Berlin, where he was involved in interviewing Nazi war criminals. After serving in the army he contracted Hepatitis C, which plagued him for the rest of his life. His children didn't understand why he felt sick so often. He married Wiltraud von Furstenberg Salm in

1969. They had two children, Maria Antonia and Karl, also known as "Ludie." Peter died in New York on March 12, 1994.

Peter drew, sketched, and painted in the back of his diaries, but he destroyed his art. "Paul and I saw his art, and he could have been a good artist," states Arturo.[29] Peter developed an interest in Native American art when six paintings from Millicent Rogers' Native American collection, through the cooperation of Mary Benjamin Rogers, were part of the "Contemporary American Indian Painting" exhibition at the U.S. National Gallery in Washington, D.C., in 1953. Dorothy Dunn, of the Santa Fe Indian School, organized this exhibition, the first of its kind. Forty-seven Native American artists were shown, including four from Taos Pueblo: Eva Mirabal, Tonita Lujan, Pop Chalee, and Chiu-Tah (Vincenti Mirabal).[30] Peter financially supported the Millicent Rogers Museum until his demise.

In 1927, six months after Millicent's divorce from the Count was final, she married the Argentinean, Arturo Peralta-Ramos, at Southampton. Millicent had met Peralta-Ramos some years before, on her trip to Paris in 1921 - 22 at one of the new clubs introducing the Argentinean Tango to chic Parisians. Their relationship did not develop until later, after she separated from the Count. The Colonel approved of the marriage and liked his new son-in-law a great deal. He gave his daughter a trust fund of $500,000, of which $30,000 per year interest would go to the young couple. For their honeymoon they sailed to South America. Millicent came back three months later with two lovebirds and a wildcat. She also brought back a lot of ancient gaucho silver.

Arturo senior was descended from a wealthy Argentinean family. The family were the founders of Mar del Plata in Argentina, a meeting place of the wealthy at the end of the nineteenth century. Patricio Peralta-Ramos, Arturo's grandfather, founded Mar del Plata in 1874. Arturo was a race-car and bobsled enthusiast, and a handsome, dashing, lucky gambler. Arturo owned, and was captain of, a bobsled team in Austria and competed in major races in Austria and Switzerland. He also did midget car racing in the USA and Hawaii.

Millicent and Arturo I in their bobsled sweaters.
(Courtesy Peralta-Ramos family archives.)

Arturo's family owned *La Razon*, the major national evening newspaper of Argentina. The family also financed the building of the race car Berta LR-V8, named "La Razon." The Berta project of building an all-Argentinean race car was born while the engineer Oreste Berta was on a European trip with Juan Manuel

Fangio, a great world champion Argentinean race driver. Also involved was Patricio Peralta-Ramos, Arturo I's grandfather, and his father, also called Arturo. Millicent and her sons retained a life-long interest and love of cars and racing.

Berta race car in Argentina, from left to right: Marcos Peralta, Luis DiPalma, Oreste Berta, Oscar Mauricio Franco, and Don Patricio Peralta-Ramos. (Courtesy http://historiadeautomovilismo.blogspot.com/)

In November 1928 Arturo Peralta-Ramos II, the son of Millicent and Arturo Peralta-Ramos, was born in Southampton, Long Island.

"At the time H. Rogers (the Colonel) decided that Arturo Peralta-Ramos I should have a job, and since Paul Shields of Shields and Company, a highly respected brokerage firm on Wall Street, was a friend of Arturo I, the Colonel transferred $500,000 to an open account at that firm in the name of H.H. Rogers. That way Arturo would learn from Shields and Company how to invest in the stock market and investment banking. Arturo I arrived at opening bell and was shown how to read stock reports by two professional stockbrokers. When the heads of the department, including Paul Shields, went to lunch, he was asked to join them at Wall Street clubs. When

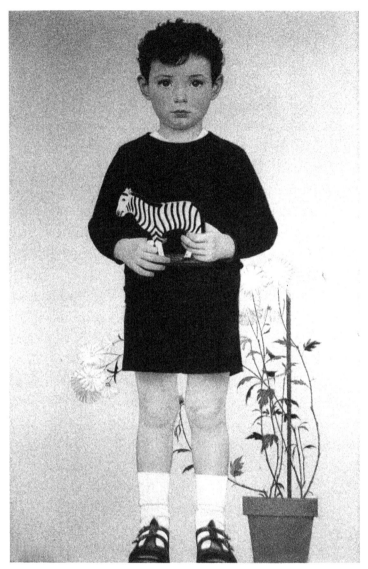

Bernard Boutet de Monvel, Portrait of Arturo Peralta-Ramos II.
(Courtesy Arturo Peralta-Ramos II.)

they left, he left. This continued for a week or so. Then one day at lunch, Paul Shields decided that Arturo I was not ever going to be a broker, so they decided to see if he could become a floor trader for the firm. After two days on the floor, it was determined that aggression was not in his make-up and he was returned to the firm's office library, where he was to study corporations they might be interested in handling. The following week Arturo I received a call from the Colonel asking him to come to dinner that night. Laughingly, the Colonel informed him that since Arturo I had an income of his own, he would set up a trust fund for Millicent, and between the two incomes they should survive very well. Arturo was pleased with the decision, and he and Millicent happily agreed that each would live off their own income.

"Arturo I went back to his previous ways and became a fixture in both the Racquet and Brook clubs and the "21" restaurant plus many joyous weekends at Mary Benjamin Rogers' beautiful house in Tuxedo Park. He and Millicent frequently went down to Southampton and stayed at the Beach House. While there he would often go over to the Port of Missing Men, approximately 15 to 20 miles on the other (North Shore) of Long Island where only men were permitted to come to shoot wild birds with the Colonel on his Cow Neck hunting preserve.

"Then lightning stuck," Arturo II relates, "Father, while looking for some papers in their library, found Mother's rollback writing chest was partially stuck open and papers were keeping it from closing. Opening the rollback, dozens of her papers came tumbling out onto the floor. Bending to put them back Father discovered they were all her unpaid monthly clothing, jewelry, handbag, and shoe bills. On and on it went. When she returned, he confronted her with the situation. Her only comment was a very uninterested, 'Oh, don't worry about those petty things, I'll get around to it sometime; and they know I'm not poor or I wouldn't have bought those necessities.' She casually left the room unperturbed by the matter. Many years later I asked my father about this, and he very casually responded, 'My son, that was your mother.'"[31]

Arturo II was very close to his dad. They belonged to the Philadelphia Gun Club, the oldest gun club in the world. They also shot all over Europe and in the U.S., South America, and Africa.

In February of 1931, in New York City, Paul Peralta-Ramos was born. This was during the Depression, and many people were desperate. According to Arturo, there was a kidnapping attempt on Peter that was thwarted at the last moment. This happened shortly before the Lindbergh kidnapping in March 1932. Fears about the family being a target for kidnappers convinced the Colonel that it was safer if they lived abroad. Millicent and her family left for Europe and lived first in a farmhouse estate of an Argentinean friend of Arturo's near Caen, France. The house had its own private zoo with wild game.

Millicent and Arturo I then moved to Gstaad, Switzerland, in 1933. They moved to the Arlberg Valley in Austria, where she initially rented a house in St. Anton. Arturo I had many friends in Austria, and they led an extensive social life. After her father's death in 1935, she used her inheritance to build a chalet in the hills above the village, where she lived until she left Austria when war broke out in September 1939. The beauty of the mountains, the simple honesty of the local people and

Bernard Boutet de Monvel, Portrait of Paul Peralta-Ramos.
(Courtesy Arturo Peralta-Ramos II.)

Millicent in the 1930's. (Courtesy Millicent Rogers Museum.)

her attraction to the new sport of downhill skiing led them to settle in this area of Austria.

Hannes Schneider founded the first major ski school in St. Anton in 1921. Schneider, who became world famous as the father of downhill skiing, developed the Arlberg System to teach skiing with both speed and safety. The sport became tremendously popular worldwide, especially among the wealthy traveling around Europe who spread tales of Schneider's techniques. By 1935 there were about 80 instructors at the Hannes Schneider Ski School. Millicent's husband, Arturo I, a champion of

Millicent's chalet in St. Anton, Austria. (Courtesy Rosmarie Matt.)

Biedermeier bed in St. Anton, later shipped to Claremont. (Courtesy Peralta-Ramos family archives.)

the two-man bobsled, had often taken Millicent down the bobsled racing runs in St. Moritz, and she was taken with the speed and thrill of it all. Millicent also became an avid downhill skier. In St. Anton, she became close friends with Schneider and many of the ski instructors, including Benno Rybizka, Otto Lang, Toni Matt, Otto Tschol, and Friedl Pfeiffer, who moved to America in the 1930's to start ski schools at all the major ski resorts that were opening to meet the growing demand for the new sport.

Rudi Matt, Millicent, and Ronald Balcom on the chalet balcony.
(Courtesy Rosmarie Matt.)

Arturo II and Paul in Austria. (Courtesy Rosmarie Matt.)

Millicent had a passionate affair with Rudi Matt, the star instructor of the school and winner of the gold medal for downhill slalom skiing at the 1936 Olympics. In December 1935, Millicent divorced Arturo in Reno. "Mother's affair with Rudi Matt was partially to blame for the divorce," states Arturo II. "My father and mother never stopped liking one another, but could not live together. They always remained friends."[32]

During the same period, Schuschnigg (Dr. Kurt von Schuschnigg, Chancellor of the First Austrian Republic) and his wife Herma often took skiing vacations in St. Anton. They became friends with Millicent, and she questioned them intensely about the political situation. They were concerned that the aggressive German moves would provoke another major war. In July 1935, Schuschnigg was injured in a car crash and his wife Herma, and their chauffeur were killed. The chauffeur had been drugged the day before the accident and the car's brake line punctured. Kurt Jr., the Chancellor's son, who was severely injured but survived the crash, had no doubt that the Nazis were responsible.[33]

At one time Paul asked his mother how she could have children with her fragile health. Her reply was, "I'm a woman and nearly every man, from the beginning of time, desires an heir. For whatever reason it is immaterial this is part of every woman's obligation. If health denies it, it is the duty of the woman to inform the man prior to marriage or she enters marriage in deceit. It is then up to the man to decide whether to proceed with the marriage."[34]

Like Peter, Arturo II's life was boarding schools with his older brother in Europe. Their first languages

were French, German, and English with a German
governess. They didn't improve their English skills until
they came to the U.S. just before World War II. The
boys spent summers with their Rogers grandmother in
Venice, Capri, and Brioni on the Adriatic Sea. Paul, being
the baby, was tutored at first. Later, when he was enrolled
at Choate, one of Paul's tutors there was John F. Joseph.
Millicent adored John and they shared a love of literature
and Greek classics. John was later Paul's best man at his
wedding and also tutored Paul's son Phillip.

John Joseph, 1952. (Courtesy Arturo Peralta-Ramos II.)

A letter sent December 20, 1984, from the Millicent Rogers Museum, written by Arturo H. Peralta-Ramos III, states, "John Joseph entered my family as a close friend of my grandmother, Millicent Rogers; tutored my uncle and father as kids; played Santa Claus to their children as they grew; guided me through Choate and continued as a close friend thereafter."[35] The library at the Millicent Rogers Museum in Taos, New Mexico, is named after John F. Joseph.

When Millicent moved Paul to Taos, she was unhappy with the quality of the schools, and she asked John to come to Taos to tutor Paul. But after visiting New Mexico in 1949, John decided not to try to break his contract with Choate and returned to Connecticut (see letter to John Paul from Millicent on page 140).

Arturo II and Paul followed the Ramos family's enthusiasm for racing. The sons were involved in U.S. sports car racing when it re-commenced after World War

Paul in a race car. (Courtesy *Life* Magazine, July 2, 1951.)

II. Millicent saw a picture of a crashed race car in *Life* magazine which depicted a young boy in the crowd hit by the car and killed. There were possibly two different photos that she may have seen. One was a Watkins Glen race through the streets and the other was the Bridgehampton. Since Paul had raced at both circuits, she became anxious and sent $500 for airfare to come home from Italy. He bought Italian shirts instead!

Paul was later in the Navy, doing military service like Peter and the Colonel, which continued the family tradition going back to the Revolutionary War. Millicent's involvement in helping the World War II effort was also part of that tradition. When Peter joined up in 1944, Millicent, concerned he might be captured, urged him to always carry a passport. She had 22K gold leaf hidden in the heels of his shoes, which she had hollowed out. She had gold army belt buckles made for him by her jeweler friend Joseph Fried. This way he always had something of value to trade for food and freedom.

Arturo II, owing to injuries he suffered from an auto accident, was not eligible for active service, but he became an expert on military relationships and espionage. Arturo married Dusty Kitterman from Virginia in December 1949 and had two children, Arturo III and a daughter, Lorian. After divorcing in 1963, Arturo married Jacqueline Blanchard in 1965. Jackie is a thoroughbred horse breeder and equestrian, and was a fashion model for some of the top designers in the U.S.

Arturo II is also artistically inclined. He studied under Reginald Marsh in New York. One day at their home in Taos, Arturo had his painting materials on the patio and the Honorable Dorothy Brett, one of Millicent's friends, was visiting. Brett was the Englishwoman who had come with D.H. Lawrence and Frieda on their second visit to Taos in 1924. Brett stayed on in Taos. She was an accomplished artist and a graduate of the Slade School in London. She asked Arturo what colors he could see, knowing he was color blind. He responded, "Black and white, but sometimes grey if it's vivid enough." Brett expressed disappointment, "Damn, I was hoping you could see the red of the leaves or the green of the tree. But, go ahead and paint."[36]

Arturo's son, Arturo III, is a professional photographer. His daughter Lorian is one of the world's foremost experts on the English artist Sir Alfred Munnings.

Of Paul's children, his son Philip is a mountain climber and a professional back country guide for outdoor adventures in Colorado. As a mountain climber, he and two close friends set the world record as the first to climb Mount Yulong and reach the 18,360-foot Shanzidou peak in Yunnan province, China. Philip spent the last four years of Paul's life with Paul, many weeks at a time, fishing with their family cousin Sergio Peralta-Ramos in Argentina. Paul's daughter Christina is an actress, wife, and model in California. Christina and Philip continue to be active on the board of the Millicent Rogers Museum in Taos. Daughter Isabella is a homemaker in Oklahoma.

Antonia, Peter's daughter, is an artist and an environmentalist active in shark research and protection. His son, Karl-Ludwig Salm, inherited the title of Count. Ludie, as he is called, is a real estate advisor.

As an avid collector of art and books, Paul was part owner of a bookstore in New York City. He was significantly helpful in bringing Roman Polanski's first feature film, the highly acclaimed *Knife in the Water* to the U.S. Paul died on August 6, 2003, and is buried in Sierra Vista Cemetery in Taos next to his mother. He had spent part of every year in Taos for 55 years. His children Christina, Isabella, and Philip survive Paul.

In January 1936, Millicent married Ronald Bush Balcom, a New York Wall Street broker, a good amateur tennis player, and a top-notch skier. Millicent and Ronald had no children and were divorced in March 1941. Peter and Arturo were put in a Swiss boarding school while Paul went with her and Ronald to Austria, where she had built the chalet. She traveled with her seven beloved dachshunds for which she had special life jackets made.

Top: Millicent and Ronald on a picnic in Austria. Bottom Left: Millicent and Ronald in front of the chalet. Bottom Right: Millicent and her dachshunds in Austria. (Courtesy Rosmarie Matt.)

In keeping with Millicent's fascination with native costumes, when she lived in Austria she adapted her wardrobe to the national dress of the Tyrol: dirndls, aprons, embroidered vests and jackets, and peaked Tyrolean hats. It is an interesting side-note that in 1937, when Wallis Simpson married the Duke of Windsor, she adapted a Tyrolean chic outfit for her honeymoon, imitating Millicent Rogers' style.

Millicent in her Tyrolean outfit. (Courtesy Millicent Rogers Museum.)

In his memoirs, the Chancellor's son, Kurt, recalled an adventure he had with Millicent and Ronald Balcom:

We were both stopped short by the arrival of Fräulein Alice. She must have heard us, but all she said was, "There you are, Rudi. Good! Let's get you settled in your room." As we turned in the direction of our rooms, Rudi gave me a noncommittal glance and shrugged his shoulders. I merely smiled; yes, we would see. Fräulein Alice had arranged for us to take lessons with two young skiers who were beginning to make names for themselves. With their growing accomplishments on the slopes, Hannes Schneider and Rudi Matt were attracting more attention to the sport. The graceful but difficult telemark skiing of Colonel Bartl's generation was now considered old-fashioned. Telemark had yielded to the new vogue for skiing fast. There was another recent development: skijoring. Fräulein Alice herself had brought up the subject and made it perfectly clear that (a) it was dangerous and (b) we were not to participate. Rudi objected immediately. "Even the brainless can hold a rope. The car does the work of pulling the skis." "No!" Without any pause whatsoever, Rudi launched an attack on another front.

Could we not at least find our own way home after lessons? Fräulein Alice graciously agreed to this seemingly innocent request. The following afternoon, as we were hoisting our skis onto our shoulders, a new American car stopped beside us. It was a shiny Ford station wagon with wood paneling. We were admiring it when out stepped Ronald Balcom and his wife, the Standard Oil heiress, Millicent Rogers. As the former wife of Count Ludwig von Salm, she was fluent in German. She had also become a friend of Austria and one of Father's supporters. "Uncle Ronni!" Rudi shouted, waving his free arm. Uncle Ronni waved back, and Aunt Millicent called out to us, "Hello Rudi! Hello Kurti! What are you two doing wandering around when you could be skiing?" We hurried to Uncle Ronni's fantastically beautiful car and his even more fantastically beautiful wife. Without missing a beat, Rudi prevaricated, "Well, it's funny that you should ask. We've been waiting for someone who was supposed to take us skijoring, but it looks like we've been let down." I did my best to keep my mouth from falling open. "Is that right?" asked Uncle Ronni. This was a comment rather than a question. They both looked at me. Late on the uptake, I nodded vigorously. "We're on our way over to Saint Christoph's for tea. Would you boys like to hitch yourselves to the back of our car and join us?" "Would we ever!"

Uncle Ronni's wife broke in here. "Ronni, darling," she observed, "do you think that's wise? It is a rather dangerous sport." Uncle Ronni glanced from his wife to us, then back at her. "But, my angel, Rudi says they've done this before. Right boys?" "Oh, many times, Uncle Ronni!" effortlessly rolled off Rudi's tongue. Not as verbally nimble, I merely continued to nod. "Good!" Uncle Ronni said, clapping us both on our backs. "There, you see, darling? They're practically professionals, and they just want to have a little fun. How can we say no?" Impervious to her good sense, he turned to us. "Put on your skis, and I'll tie the ropes to the back bumper." It was amazing that Uncle Ronni had ropes. I simply could not imagine Aunt Millicent skijoring, nor could I picture her allowing Uncle Ronni to do so. But Rudi and I needed no more urging; we hurriedly put on our skis. I did have a vaguely disturbing feeling about it though. What if Fräulein Alice found out? As we picked up our ropes I said to Rudi, "That was a whopping big lie!" Unimpressed, Rudi arched his eyebrows at me and said, "And just who is the beneficiary of that?" "You boys all set?" called Uncle Ronni from his window. "All set, Uncle Ronni!" we chorused. Before one could think twice we were off. Aunt Millicent had turned herself around in her seat and watched with an expression of concern. I ignored it because I needed every bit of concentration that I could muster just to keep my balance. Uncle Ronni could not have driven at much more than a slow crawl, but to us it felt as if we were taking those curves at fifty miles an hour. I had just begun to feel faint stirrings of confidence when, completely without warning, Rudi deliberately slammed sideways into me. Then, laughing maniacally, he swung back to his side. Had I been able to risk freeing one hand, I certainly would have punched him. By the grace of God, I did just manage to stay upright. As I was contemplating retaliation, Aunt Millicent called out, "Stop that!", while vigorously shaking her head back and forth and wagging her finger at us. And so we did. By the time the Ford station wagon pulled up in front of the hotel in Saint Christoph, the ropes were frozen solid in my hands. It might have been the cold, but it could easily have been the grip of fear. I was pleased to see that Rudi was in exactly the same state. Still, we had been on the ride of our lives! "There! You see, Millicent? Professional skijorers!" Uncle Ronni jumped out of the car and cuffed each of us on the shoulder. "Well done! Did you enjoy it?" Through frozen lips we articulated our assent as well as we could, but our enthusiasm was unmistakable. "Come on, boys," he laughed, untying the ropes and helping us out of our skis, "put everything in the car, then come inside and we'll have tea." He took Aunt Millicent's arm and led her into the hotel. As we followed them, I had one thought firmly in mind: I was motoring back.

Rudi was sitting on the backseat beside me when we pulled up to the Post Hotel. Hoping to slip in unnoticed, I asked Uncle Ronni to let us out at the hotel's main entrance, instead of at the annex. It was all for naught. There, clearly visible, was the waiting form of Fräulein Alice. Our lesson was to have ended some two hours ago. I did not want to guess how long she had been waiting out there. Rudi and I looked at each other for a long moment then climbed out of the car. Fräulein Alice introduced herself to Aunt Millicent and Uncle Ronni. "We had an excellent afternoon, didn't we, boys?" said Uncle Ronni. "Oh yes!" we sang out, as we scrambled to unload our *skis. I knew I needed a miracle, the sort where Fräulein Alice did not find out about the skijoring. Aunt Millicent said, "How careless of us not to have had the boys call you. I'm so sorry." Hoping to prevent discussion between Fräulein Alice and the Balcoms, I blurted out, "Fräulein Alice, Uncle Ronni and Aunt Millicent took us to Saint Christoph for tea. Rudi and I had three different kinds of Kuchen (cake), but it doesn't matter because we could still eat a cow, we're so hungry." Clatter, clatter—down went skis and poles, a desperate diversionary tactic. Fräulein Alice was bending to help me pick them up when Uncle Ronni chose, most unfortunately, to boast of our prowess. "Bet you didn't know what experts these boys are at skijoring!" Before I could blink, Rudi—the coward—sang out his thanks and auf wiedersehen-ed his way into the Annex, tossing his skis and poles against the wall as he went inside. I hadn't the courage to look at Fräulein Alice. To her enormous credit, she graciously thanked the couple, saying not a word about my being forbidden to go skijoring. "Give me the skis, Kurt." It was bad when she called me Kurt. I obeyed, all the while avoiding her eye, but Fräulein Alice was not so easily evaded. "Stand still and look at me." This was more than bad; it was very bad. "You know what you did today was seriously wrong, don't you?" "Fräulein Alice, all we did was. . ." I was brusquely cut off. "This is not a discussion concerning Rudi. I am concerned that you do what you are supposed to do. Equally important, that you don't do what you're not supposed to do. Now you come with me." I meekly followed her straight to Rudi's door. He must have had his ear pressed against it because he opened immediately at Fräulein Alice's knock. From the expression on his face it was clear that he had expected it to be me, alone. "Rudi, I have told Kurt, and now I am telling you. Kurt is strictly forbidden to go skijoring again. Is that perfectly clear?" "Yes, Fräulein Alice." He had the good sense to look chastened. "And before you or Kurt", here I got another direct look, "even consider going somewhere without my knowledge, you*

had better first give thought to what the results of your actions will be.
Is that perfectly clear?" This implied threat of informing his mother
was the one effective weapon against Rudi. "Yes, Fräulein Alice", we
said together. "Very well. Now both of you change for dinner." After
we had once again said, "Yes, Fräulein Alice", she disappeared into
her room. Rudi and I grimaced at one another. He sighed silently and
mimed the act of wiping perspiration from his brow with the back
of his hand. I gave him a shove and mouthed the word coward. His
only response was an exaggerated shrug of his shoulders. Really, we
both had gotten off the hook lightly. We ducked into our rooms, and
in no time reappeared: changed, spotless, and on our best behavior.
Fräulein Alice really was a genius at managing us boys.[37]

In January 1938, the boys went back to school in Switzerland, and Millicent and Ronald travelled to Paris, where her mother maintained a house. At that time Paris was not only the center of fashion, but also the world leader in elegant, streamlined, coach-built automobiles. The latest models were shown every November at the Paris Salon held in the Grand Palais. Millicent and her second husband had owned a Mercedes 500K, an elegant and expensive touring car.

While in Paris, Millicent and Ronald purchased one of the finest French touring cars, a 1937 Delage D8-120 Aérosport Coupe (chassis #51623), with a custom coach-built body by Letourneur & Marchand. Economically, 1937 had been a difficult year for Delage, so the company must have been very pleased when Millicent Rogers purchased the Aérosport shortly after the show. According to Millicent's son Arturo, Ronald first saw the car at the 1937 Paris Salon or shortly afterward. He believed that the car's superb, innovative design would appeal to his wife's great sense of style. Millicent agreed, with one minor modification. She thought that the rear fender shapes were not in keeping with the elegance of the car's overall design and asked that they be lowered to make a longer, sleeker look.

The car was returned to Letourneur & Marchand. To make these modifications, the rear body sheet metal was removed and the wood body structure exposed. The rear fenders were hung temporarily on the wood body. In April 1938, when he was on spring break, Arturo recalled going to see the Delage with his mother, younger brother, and Ronald Balcom at Letourneur & Marchand's atelier in Paris and vividly remembered his mother taking out her lipstick and drawing the exact shape she wanted on the rear fender sheet metal. Several months later, when that work was completed and the sheet metal reinstalled, the car was repainted a darker metallic grey, as Millicent had specified. Eventually Millicent had the Delage shipped to her next home Claremont Manor in Virginia, where it remained until 1949.

Side view of Millicent's Delage D8-120 Aerosport Coupe #51623 taken outside the Paris Salon, October 1937. (Courtesy Archives of *Les Amis de Delage*, France via David Cooper.)

Millicent had a serious heart attack in Paris in 1938. She was 36 years old. Friends and family rushed to her side. When the doctors came out after examining her, they told Mary Benjamin that Millicent was probably paralyzed and it was unlikely that she would ever walk again or continue any of her usual activities. Millicent overheard the doctors' dire prognosis. Her son Arturo remembers the French doors opening loudly, and Millicent standing in the doorway in her nightgown, bluntly telling the doctors, "Fuck you." Then, exhausted, she fell and had to be carried back to bed. Despite the doctors' predictions, she recovered. She would not be daunted by her illness. That was the beginning of Millicent wearing heavy bracelets, which she designed and made up in 18K gold. The weight of them exercised her debilitated arms.

"'She knew how to take her faults and make herself stunning," her youngest son, Paul Peralta-Ramos, told *Vogue*. He pronounced his mother, 'a compelling beauty in spite of her 'big-knuckled hands' and 'gaunt' visage. The hefty bracelets she adopted, for instance, were basically glamorous barbells that forced her to exercise her troubled limb.'"[38]

Millicent made sure her boys studied yoga and meditation to keep them as healthy as possible, especially since Paul, like her, was prone to illness. When the boys were ill, she put herself and them in meditative trances to rest.

Millicent, anticipating the coming war and fearing the worst, spent the fall of 1938 in the U.S. making arrangements to move back to the States. She placed her two younger sons in school for a term at Tuxedo Park.

The family returned again to Europe in December 1938 and spent Christmas in Paris with Millicent's mother. In January 1939 Millicent's sons returned to school in Switzerland and she returned to Austria to make arrangements to close down her house there as the Nazis were occupying Austria.

After their usual summer in Italy, and with the return of imminent war scares, Millicent sent her sons back to the United States in August 1939 on the ship *New Amsterdam*, arriving in New York on September 1, 1939. During the voyage the ship was stopped by a German submarine and several people were taken off. The passengers were ordered off the deck and warned not to take any photographs of the submarine, but Arturo II secretly took some with his Kodak Brownie. His photos revealed the submarine's number on the conning tower. Years later his photographs were compared to German Naval logs to determine the identity of the passengers who were removed. The photos were entered as evidence during the Nuremburg Trials.[39]

War broke out on September 1, 1939, with Germany invading Poland. On September 3, Britain and France declared war on Germany, honoring their treaty obligations to Poland. Millicent and her husband Ronald left Europe on the *Statendam* on September 5th. Knowing that German submarines were already prevalent and fearing that the Germans had mined the harbors, the crew refused to board without extra hazard pay. A standoff ensued, resolved when the passengers, including Millicent and Ronald, agreed to take over many of the crew's duties. During the voyage, the *Statendam* was diverted to pick up British survivors from a merchant marine ship that had been attacked by a German submarine. The *Statendam* arrived in New York on September 14, 1939.

Arturo II relates, "After her divorce from Ronald Balcom, she (Mother) had learned her lesson. She was too dramatic, restless, and imaginative–and far too liberated–to be bound by any one relationship. Marriage was stagnation and complacency for her. Her biggest problem was that she knew more about most subjects than the men she knew. The men she found physically attractive were not usually the best intellectual companions. Many of her later lovers, Forrestal, Dahl, Fleming and Gable, could hold their own with her."[40]

Millicent was a blunt speaker in spite of her reserve and soft voice. Of men she said she believed in pillow talk, and that she didn't think she should destroy a man's ego. She also declared that every powerful man had a mistress on the side who controlled him. She told this to Arturo when he knocked on her bedroom door to go in to chat with her. The boys were always welcome by Millicent into her room when they knocked as she was often in bed, not feeling well.

Paul was quoted in an article in *New Mexico Magazine*, "The Count was a nice guy. They couldn't get along. My father, a nice guy. They couldn't get along. As for Ronnie Balcom, a really nice guy. They couldn't get along…"[41]

"My mother didn't cook, but she collected recipes. She had three volumes of recipes for her cooks," says Arturo. "She liked eggs and ate them prepared in many different ways. She also loved wine. My father was a wine connoisseur, so she learned fine wines from him."[42] Christina Lucia Peralta-Ramos Luera is currently writing a cookbook based on her grandmother's recipes.

Michael D. Coe, a cousin of Millicent's, states in his article, "Not surprisingly, a number of manuscript recipe books from the Rogerses, Giffords, and the Huttlesons (the family of H.H. Rogers' mother) have survived, and some of these recipes have 18th and even 17th century dates. The copies which we have are typescripts prepared for our cousin Millicent Rogers (1904–1963 sic 1902-1953), apparently some time in the 1940s. The oft-married Millicent was a remarkable woman, whose elegant beauty and outstanding taste in clothes established her as one of the fashion trendsetters of her day; she was also a talented designer of jewelry (Dame Edith Sitwell would wear her creations only), and the founder of an important Indian museum bearing her name, located in Taos, New Mexico. Beneath her sophisticated high style, Millicent was a warm and down-to-earth woman, who loved to cook, and the survival of these recipes should be credited to her. (Son Arturo corrected this statement by noting, 'Millicent didn't cook, but took a keen interest in the food served in her homes.')"[43]

Dame Edith Sitwell inscribed a copy of a collection of aphorisms on the art of poetry, *A Poet's Notebook* 1943, "For Mrs. Millicent Rogers, Your Golden kindness from her grateful Edith Sitwell." Millicent made a large necklace for Edith. Edith says of her Aztec necklace, "This gold necklace was made for me by an American woman called Millicent Rogers. She was one of my greatest friends, though I only met her once. She sent it to me, and the British Museum kept it for four days and thought it was Pre-Columbian, undoubtedly from the tomb of an Inca–though they couldn't make out how the gold could be stiffened in a way that wasn't in existence in those days. But I have to be careful of the clanking when I am reciting and don't wear it often for that."[44]

Millicent in a 1949 letter to the Honorable Dorothy Brett records, "The Sitwells were in town (New York City) and did the Façade at the Museum of Modern Art. But the mechanics were bad – Otherwise I thought it very charming–and the poems lovely–I thought her cosy and great fun."[45]

Dame Edith Sitwell wearing the necklace Millicent made for her. (Courtesy *The Last Years of a Rebel: a Memoir of Edith Sitwell* by Elizabeth Salter.)

WAR YEARS

After she recovered from her heart attack, Millicent returned to Austria in late spring 1938. The situation in Austria had turned grave. On March 12th the Germans marched in and occupied Austria, an event known as the Anschluss, declaring it henceforth to be part of a unified German State. She saw for herself the brutality of the Nazi regime as it began initiating persecution measures against Austria's Jews, including a number of Millicent's friends.

"'She was arrested twice right after the Anschluss,' her son Paul said. 'She had a huge American flag made in Switzerland and flew it from this bloody tall pole (at her home in St. Anton). And when Hitler's henchmen ordered her to take it down, she refused. 'Whatever for?' she said. 'We're not at war with you.' My mother had the kind of guts you don't see anymore.'"[46]

Austrian Nazi storm troopers came a second time and again ordered her to take the flag down. This time Millicent told them that the flag was on American soil. The Nazis troopers looked at each other quizzically, saluted, and left. Later, Millicent did take the flag down after advice from friends that since she was aiding in smuggling her Jewish friends out, she better not call attention to herself.

Millicent realized that the Nazis were not going to let her take any of her assets out of the country. Anticipating the problem, she purposely paid none of the bills sent to her there; and she also assumed the responsibility for bills owed by her neighbors. "Those large, unpaid bills piled up for more than twelve months… An Austrian Nazi official purchased her chalet (in St. Anton) and gleefully informed Mrs. Balcom that the purchase money could not be taken out of the country. But she merely applied that money to the payment of all those unpaid bills, and the accounts are even."[47]

Once again Millicent was taking on the Boche as she did in her diary entry as a young woman for WWI (pg. 7). She plunged passionately into activities related to the war.

At the beginning of the war in Europe, Churchill sent his friend William Stephenson to the United States to set up an organization, later known as British Security Coordination (BSC), with a mission to share intelligence with the Americans, protect British interests, and influence American opinion to the British side. The ultimate goal, which had to be approached surreptitiously due to America's neutrality and isolationism, was to bring America into the war to fight against the Nazis alongside the British.

One BSC tactic was to set up front organizations headed by prominent Americans with important social connections to support British causes. It is likely that Millicent Rogers was asked to head one such front organization, because in August 1940, she founded and became executive director of the Medical and Surgical Relief Committee (MSRC), which operated until May

1947. As a result, Millicent spent a good part of the World War II years in Washington, D.C. Millicent was personally responsible for raising over a million dollars, in addition to millions more from personal friends.

Arturo II always wondered how his mother got involved with this work. She did not know much about medicine and did not have many friends who were doctors. Millicent's reputation in social and fashion circles gave no indication of her ability to run a complex organization. But she was well positioned to access information and influence. She was close friends with a number of people who were significant in the intelligence community, including Sir William Wiseman (British Intelligence liaison during World War I, later a partner at Kuhn, Loeb), Hamish Mitchell (British Intelligence in the U.S. just before the war), Vincent Astor (who provided private intelligence to Roosevelt), William Stephenson (head of the BSC), Lord Lothian (the British ambassador), James Forrestal (later U.S. Secretary of the Navy), William Donovan (who later was head of the OSS, the American intelligence agency established during the war), Ian Fleming (British Navy intelligence officer and later author of the James Bond books), and Ivar Bryce and Roald Dahl (both BSC intelligence agents). Dahl was later to become the acclaimed children's author of such books as *Charlie and the Chocolate Factory*. It is likely that Stephenson, freshly arrived in New York approached William Wiseman, Hamish Mitchell, Ivar Bryce and Vincent Astor for advice. All three of them knew many prominent Americans, knew Millicent personally, knew of her experiences in Austria and would have suggested her to Stephenson.

Millicent in her 68th Street, New York apartment wearing a Valentina brocade wrap, 1940's. (Courtesy, *Vogue* Magazine.)

Millicent was the owner of Claremont Manor in Virginia, which she bought in 1940, after returning from Austria. As a result of her friendship with James Forrestal, Secretary of Navy, Claremont Manor was used to rehabilitate injured naval aviators from 1942 to 1945. "The book *Claremont Manor* does confirm in one sentence that the owner of the property during WWII, Millicent Rogers (a very wealthy person), was a personal friend of Forrestal and that Forrestal did ask Rogers to accept the aviators (which she apparently did)."[48]

James Forrestal and Millicent were good friends as well as lovers. Arturo Peralta-Ramos said of Forrestal, "Of all of her lovers I liked Forrestal and Dahl best." Arturo also said Forrestal was at Millicent's a lot during this time period (1940–1947).

"Forrestal liked the company of good-looking women, women of style and manners, brainy women; but if he found real joy in this, those of us who were close to him never observed it. …He enjoyed his successes with ladies, but he did not really love anyone. Because he was in the main discreet and secretive, it is not easy to identify the various women in his life during the Washington period, classify them as lovers or merely sharers of a cocktail or afternoon tea. He would drop by in the late afternoon or following some official reception dinner. Or he would draw close friends into a delicate conspiracy. 'Dear Dan,' he wrote to his friend Dan Caulkins, 'I will be stopping by your house this evening after work, about nine o'clock. Mrs. So-and-so (his current lady) will be there. Thank you for having her. Jim.'"[49]

Forrestal, son of an Irish immigrant, was born in 1892. He went to Princeton in 1912, but left without a degree, lacking one hour of credit. He qualified as a pilot in WWI, but didn't see active service. In 1940 Roosevelt appointed Forrestal as an advisor. In August 1940 he was appointed Under Secretary of Navy. He then became the new Secretary of the Navy in April 1944 when William Knox died. He held that post until 1947, when he became Secretary of Defense. Truman was unhappy with his performance and forced him to leave on March 28, 1949.

Soon afterwards, suffering from depression, he was admitted to Bethesda (Naval) Hospital. In May he was found, having fallen from the 16th floor. Forrestal's two sons, his brother Henry, and Arturo II all remain convinced that he was pushed from the window. They have no concrete proof, but knowing Forrestal's habits, and a book opened where he was last reading and making notes, it seems unlikely to them that he committed suicide. To this day Forrestal's death remains a mystery as to whether it was a murder conspiracy or a suicide. News of the death was instantaneous on the radio and in the newspapers, so Millicent was probably informed by the radio if not by her sons or a close friend. Arturo II does not remember her reaction at the time.

When she was forced to leave her house in St. Anton, Millicent had to get all of her belongings out. "Millicent had her extensive collection of Biedermeier furniture, her art collection and her Delage Aérosport shipped from Europe to Claremont Manor. 'I consider it a desecration in Virginia to change even one single architectural detail,' Millicent told Billy Baldwin. 'Inside you can do whatever you want because that is entirely up to you; you're going to see it, and you're responsible.' From St. Anton in Austria she brought decorative porcelain stoves. From France she imported her Watteau, Fragonard and Boucher drawings. This house became a jewel box filled with treasures that reflected her eclectic taste-her collection of antique clocks, a desk that once belonged to the poet Schiller…"[50]

Millicent converted Claremont into a working farm, while also housing the naval aviators, and continued to work closely with Forrestal. She wanted it to be a self-supporting working farm so that, if the United States entered the war, it would be exempt from rationing. She also began stockpiling supplies in anticipation of shortages. She had large containers of soap and glycerin stored in preparation for the coming war. She ordered brand-new tractors, trucks, generators, horses, sheep, pigs, chickens, and beef and milking cows.

Claremont Manor was one of the great houses in the Tidewater area of Virginia. Arturo Peralta-Ramos adds, "Her homes were like canvases that she created, perfection in period homes as were her gardens.[51] The Claremont and the Jamaican houses had ghosts. Millicent said that the ghosts get upset when the winds blow. It is an old story that a Union soldier was caught meeting a Confederate girl who was an inhabitant of Claremont, and was hanged on a large oak tree beside the President's Room window."

Claremont Manor was originally built in 1760. "Surprisingly, Claremont Manor is not on the (Historical) Registry, nor does it appear that it has ever been nominated. We find this odd given the age of Claremont Manor (the property dates back to the 1600s), the ongoing historic work at the site, and the fact that Thomas Jefferson designed some of the buildings."[52]

Guests in Claremont over the years signed their names on guest room windows, including President Abraham Lincoln, Thomas Jefferson, Hopewell, and numerous others. During the Civil War gunboats were sailing up the James River to besiege Petersburg, a major Confederate stronghold. As they sailed up the James,

Left Top: Millicent with her son Paul; *Right Top:* Millicent with her 3 sons at Claremont, Peter Salm, Paul Peralta-Ramos, Millicent, and Arturo Peralta-Ramos II. (Courtesy Arturo Peralta-Ramos II.) *Bottom:* Claremont Manor. (Courtesy *Claremont Manor* by Eve S. Gregory.)

the gunboats were also shelling mansions owned by Confederate families, but Lincoln ordered Claremont Manor spared owing to buildings designed on the land by Thomas Jefferson.

In Millicent's letter to Hon. Dorothy Brett on Christmas Day, 1948, she wrote about Claremont:

Dear Brett:

Merry Christmas! Really I'm sorry you didn't come here with me. It's really Beautiful, I always forget how beautiful. Today is snowing! The little fall of snow covers the lawn and the Box Hedges and the heads and shoulders of the stone Girls, the Hollys are very green on the grass still. The Red Berrys and gray-Brown trunks of Crepe-Myrtle and the Black Brown trunks of ___(handwriting undecipherable), the light green of magnolias stand out starkly on the mistyness from the River and the mistyness. There is a little wind and the snow blows leftward. Have big fires in the fire places. The rooms have dark corners in the mistyness from outside, so that the fires are Red and ...orange shadows in the rooms. The ceilings are dark too, and you can walk quietly in the rooms; I feel at home here too. It is very quiet and the River is very gray and close to it very cold. Because of Taos I feel at Home in a way I have not felt before. Before this house was built there was a Pueblo in Taos against the Mountain. There was a North house and a South house and the water between...

My Paulus and His friend ... have a lovely time sticking their noses in all the scent bottles of the dressing table. Have managed to knock over two – result the Room stinks of Chanel 5 and several other mixtures. ... Well, the Kidney seems quite good for the moment (keep fingers cross) But as the snow is lacking Paul & Arturo have decided not to go skiing which means I finish all their holidays with them till the 8th of Jan. It is quiet here the snow falling outs (outside) the ground make a little swishing sound that runs along the Earth like a whisper – and John J. (Joseph) is playing Bach

    So long now – Happy Christmas to all of you …
Kiss to the Mountain.

    Much Love, Millicent
    P.S. This place has an Isak Dinesen quality about it. It has set down in America by mistake. It was set down for a night and they forgot to pick it up again. …[53]

Eve Gregory, in her book *Claremont Manor*, states, "She (Millicent) traveled internationally and brought politicians, movie stars, and museum quality paintings and furniture to Claremont. At the same time she was kind and generous to her employees and friendly with people in town. She invited the local children to swim in the pool she had built and spoke to everyone on the road when she walked to the post office from Claremont Manor."[54]

During the war Millicent had a parrot named Sebastian as one of her pets at Claremont. "MR's maid and life-long friend Hilda Fagin (a 1924 Olympic swimmer from Norway whom Millicent met through Arturo I and his Argentinean compadres) heard the parrot, who could completely imitate Mother's voice screaming over and over again, 'Hilda – HILDAA – HILDAAA!' Knowing MR was out, and that the parrot was calling for MR, Hilda ignored the screeching parrot. When MR returned and entered the bathroom, she found Sebastian stuck in the toilet, sadly drowned!"[55]

"Clark Gable visited Claremont, but the rumor that he swam nude in the swimming pool is more titillating than likely. It is true that he was interested in buying Four Mile Tree, a plantation downriver from Claremont, but he could not persuade Nick Carter to sell." [56]

Concurrently Millicent submerged herself in the Medical and Surgical Relief Committee. She submitted, in December 1941, a design for an emblem pin for the Medical and Surgical Relief Committee of America.

Dec. 30, 1941.   M. R. BALCOM   Des. 130,930

EMBLEM PIN

Filed Oct. 24, 1941

Millicent's design for an emblem pin for the Medical and Surgical Relief Committee of America. (Courtesy Arturo Peralta-Ramos II.)

"Mrs. Huttleston Rogers (Mary Benjamin), the former Millicent Rogers, Chairman of the Medical and Surgical Relief Committee of America, today (November 12, 1942) presented emergency field operating kits to the Naval Air Station at Norfolk and to Dr. Millard Hanson, Richmond's health officer. … Each set consists of portable cases containing a wide variety of surgical instruments, medicines, antiseptics, and lanterns and dry cell batteries to provide light in a blackout. … The work began when Mrs. Rogers appealed to physicians for samples and used instruments. '…At the time England was bombed,' Mrs. Rogers said, 'We have shipped to the Free Fight French at Matequi in France, Brazzaville, and to Australia, Burma, and China, as well as to numerous occupied European nations. We were the first to send supplies to Pearl Harbor. …'"[57]

In 1945 the Medical and Surgical Relief Committee presented Millicent with a bracelet of 25 emblems donated by the 23 organizations to which the Medical and Surgical Relief Committee had extended help. In 1947, when Millicent resigned from the Medical and Surgical Relief Committee, she received thank-you letters from Madame Chiang Kai-shek, President Roosevelt, Mrs. Eleanor Roosevelt, Admiral Halsey, General William Donovan, O.S.S, General Chenault, James Forrestal, Senator William Fulbright, Admiral Zacarias, William Randolph Hearst, General Charles DeGaulle, and Lord Halifax. The family book containing these letters disappeared in 1953. She turned down the Legion'd Honor medal from France and from numerous other nations.

Millicent in her Medical and Surgical Relief Uniform.
(Courtesy Arturo Peralta-Ramos II.)

In addition to its very impressive public accomplishments, Millicent's MSRC may also have been a cover for covert activities. Millicent facilitated secret meetings between various people engaged in clandestine war work. She volunteered the use of her apartment in New York to BSC agents Roald Dahl and Ian Flemming for their use.[58]

Arturo II remembered one unusual instance when he came to New York to stay in his mother's apartment at 18 E. 68th Street. He and his brothers had been taught by Millicent that if they entered a room and there were guests, they were to say "hello" and then leave. As Arturo entered the door, he recognized a number of people in the smoke-filled room and went to greet them. Millicent rushed up, barred him from entering, and abruptly told him to leave the apartment. Later she explained that she had been hosting an important meeting of the Medical

MEDICAL AND SURGICAL RELIEF COMMITTEE, INC.

GRAYBAR BUILDING

420 LEXINGTON AVENUE

NEW YORK 17, N. Y.

TELEPHONE
MUrray Hill 9-0278

March 22, 1948

Mrs. Huttleston Rogers
18 E. 68th St.
New York 21, N. Y.

Dear Mrs. Rogers:

Gifford A. Cochran, I am very happy to announce, has been appointed Executive Director of the Medical and Surgical Relief Committee. He is serving on a volunteer basis. He brings to this work valuable experience gained in aiding Red Cross campaigns, plus first hand knowledge of the urgent need for medical and surgical supplies abroad acquired while serving in Africa and Europe over three years with the United States Army.

I believe you will also be interested in a brief report of the Committee progress since its reorganization in October 1947. We have received so far medical, surgical and dental supplies from manufacturers, physicians and hospitals, valued at more than $230,000. Individuals have contributed $26,000 in cash. Although these contributions represent but a small part of what is needed, they are a good start in the right direction.

I know you will find satisfaction in the thought that the Committee is still serving distressed people overseas from suffering and death. Such work builds up an appreciation of America throughout the world, which is needed today as never before.

Sincerely yours,

W. F. Halsey

Fleet Admiral William F. Halsey, USN (Ret.)

A copy of the letter from Admiral Halsey. (Courtesy Arruro Peralta-Ramos II.)

`MR

C O P Y   C O P Y

HEADQUARTERS OF THE GENERALISSIMO
CHINA

Chungking, Szechuan
15 July, 1942

Mrs. Rogers Balcom, Executive Chairman
Medical and Surgical Relief Committee of America
New York City, New York
United States of America

Dear Mrs. Balcom:

Upon his return from furlough, Dr. R. Gordon Agnew told me of the invaluable
work which the Medical and Surgical Relief Committee of America, under your
leadership, is doing. I should like you, and all your fellow members to know that
we are fully appreciative of the energy and enthusiasm the Committee has shown
in despatching medical supplies to China.

I would be invidious, when China has received relief in so many shapes
from well-wishers abroad to single out any one for special remark, but the pro-
vision of sadly-needed medical supplies has undoubtedly been one of the most
valuable forms that this good-will has taken. From the very beginning we were
badly lacking, not only in drugs, but in instruments and even the simplest
appliances which are a commonplace in the smallest hospitals in America.

Please tell all those associated with you how much we appreciate your goodwill
and sympathy.

Yours sincerely,

(signed) Mayling Soong Chiang

(Madame Chiang Kai-shek)

MCK-s/pc

A copy of the letter from Madam Chiang Kai-shek. (Courtesy Arturo Peralta-Ramos II.)

and Surgical Relief Committee. Arturo never could understand why a meeting of the MSRC would have been secret. He thought that perhaps the participants might not have wanted to be seen together. Afterwards, his mother refused to talk about it. Later, Arturo mentioned it to Paul, joking, "MR must think she is Mata Hari."

Adding to this information, Arturo states that during the war years his grandmother, Mary Benjamin Rogers, bought a house in Washington, D.C., at 2458 Wyoming Avenue. This house was used for private confidential meetings, and gave the family a base of operations in D.C. When the war ended, the house was promptly sold. Mary Benjamin Rogers also established the Officer's Club in Washington, D.C., which was a convenient and private place for American and British officers to meet and exchange information. Millicent Rogers frequently traveled to Washington and New York for short trips during the war years.

Although Millicent never discussed it with him, Arturo II was aware that she was instrumental in helping a number of her Jewish friends escape from Austria after the Anschluss. Through her mother, Mary Benjamin Rogers, Millicent knew Count Ciano, the son-in-law of Mussolini, in Italy. Piecing the story together years later, Arturo II believed that Millicent asked Ciano to furnish her with forty passports and travel visas so that the refugees could travel through Switzerland and Italy to Naples. The funds for this came from the Rogers family, authorized by the Hanover Bank. Through her friend Margaret Mallory, whose father owned the Clyde-Mallory shipping lines, she arranged to have a ship waiting in Naples to take the refugees to the United States.

Millicent didn't forget her skiing friends in St. Anton. Arturo II cites that Millicent returned to Austria several months later (after leaving for Paris) and saw for herself the brutality of the Nazi regime as it took over Austria and immediately initiated persecution measures against Austria's Jews, including a number of Millicent's friends. Arturo remembers seeing the Austrian Nazis threaten their opponents and desecrate the Hannes Schneider Ski School building. The Anschluss divided the ski instructors at Hannes Schneider's school, some favoring the Nazis and some opposed. Many were forced to flee the country for their political or religious beliefs.

Through her contacts, Millicent helped arrange for many of the ski instructors to leave Austria and find refuge in the United States. Hannes Schneider himself, whose anti-Nazi sympathies were well known, was arrested, transferred to Garmisch, Germany, and held under house arrest for the next year. Ultimately, Schneider and his family were ransomed from the Nazis and brought to the United States by Harvey Dow Gibson, president of Manufacturers Trust, where 90% of the Rogers family money was held. Schneider became the head of the ski school at the Cranmore Mountain Resort, New Hampshire, and later during the War helped train the American Skiing Forces in the 10th Mountain Division.[59]

Millicent's friend cum family member, Van Day Truex, "…helped to raise money to enable the distribution of medical supplies in the war zones of Europe and Asia." [60] "After America entered the war, he also went often with Rogers and her family to Claremont Manor, her Tidewater estate in Virginia. On one of his first visits there, she commissioned him to decorate the house to accommodate the Biedermeier furniture that she had shipped back from Austria (on his advice) in 1938."[61]

Millicent was a passionate woman. Her passion was expressed in her charitable work, her art, and her affairs with exceptional, strong, intelligent, handsome men. The war years brought Millicent's humanitarian activities to a passionate high. Her involvement with a variety of men also began in this period.

Her public affairs possibly began after her divorce from Balcolm in 1941, with her name being linked with at least two dashing British men, Ian Fleming and Roald Dahl. "My mother never knew, with her rheumatic fever, whether she would ever wake up in the morning, and so she lived her life to the fullest and occasionally went wild," states her son Arturo.[62]

Roald Dahl was shipped to the British Embassy in Washington D.C., as Assistant Air Attache in 1942 after being demobilized from the Royal Air Force having been injured in a downed plane during training in Libya. William Stephenson, the Canadian known among the spy ring as "Intrepid," tapped him to be a part of the British spy organization, British Security Coordination.

It was in D.C. that Dahl began writing his first short stories. "C.S. Forrester had asked Dahl to write down some RAF anecdotes so that he could shape them into a story. When Forester sat down to read what Dahl had given him, he decided to publish it exactly as it was. 'The original title of the article was "Shot Down Over Libya", now published as "A Piece of Cake" -the title was changed to sound more dramatic."[63] Dahl inscribed a copy of his first children's book, *The Gremlins*, to Mary

Roald Dahl in RAF uniform with Ernest Hemingway, May 29, 1944.
(Courtesy Corbis Images.)

Benjamin and Millicent, "I'm sorry I left so early, January 6, 1943."

According to Jennet Conant, in Washington, "…all Dahl had to do was keep up a cheerful front and eavesdrop his way through the yawning Sunday breakfasts, hunt breakfasts, luncheons, teas, tea dances, innumerable drinks, parties, banquets and not infrequent balls."[64]

"Soon Dahl was hobnobbing with Eleanor Roosevelt during weekends at Hyde Park, where he also met the president, allowing him to become, Conant expansively concludes, 'a back-channel conduit of information' to Churchill."[65]

"Eleanor Roosevelt had been reading *The Gremlins*, one of Dahl's many successful children's books, to her grandchildren. When she heard that the author was in Washington, she invited him to dinner with the President.

"'I was working entirely for Bill Stephenson then,' Dahl later said. 'My job was to try and oil the wheels between the British and the Americans. After that first dinner with the President, I used to go out to Hyde Park at weekends. There were always Roosevelts there, and people like Henry Morgenthau. I was able to ask pointed questions and get equally pointed replies because, theoretically, I was a nobody.

"'For instance, there might be some argument officially between London and Washington about future operations. I could ask FDR over lunch what he thought, and he could tell me quite openly, far more than he could say in a formal way. Bleeding this information on the highest level from the Americans was not for nefarious purposes, but for the war effort. That's why Bill planted fellows like us.'

"Roosevelt knew that the young RAF officer was yet another informal channel to Stephenson. It was part of the game never to make formal acknowledgement of this. 'I'd walk into FDR's little side room on a Sunday morning in Hyde Park and he'd be making Martinis, as he always did. And I would say "Good Morning, Mr. President." And we'd pass the time of day. He treated me as just a friend of Eleanor. And he'd say, naïvely, as if I was nobody much and he was making idle gossip, "I had an interesting communication from Winston today…."

"In this way, questions were posed and answered that, officially raised, might cause trouble. None doubted the absolute security of Stephenson's communications. They were, as Donovan was to say, the only communications for a time that were as leak proof as human endeavor could make them. It was for this reason that Donovan himself played the game and became in his turn a man 'put in place' by the unseen coordinator of intelligence in New York, knowing the President himself approved."[66]

Dahl was purposely seated next to Congresswoman Clare Boothe Luce at a dinner party. "According to (Creekmore) Fath, Dahl groaned: 'I'm all fucked out. That goddam woman has absolutely screwed me from one end of the room to another for three goddam nights.' Dahl claimed he had gone back to the ambassador that morning and attempted to plead his case: 'You know it's a great assignment, but I just can't go on…' and the Ambassador said, 'Roald did you see the Charles Laughton movie of Henry VIII?' When Dahl said yes, Halifax continued: "Well, do you remember the scene with Henry going into the bedroom with Anne of Cleves, and he turns and says, "the things I've done for England"? Well, that's what you've got to do, just close your eyes and think of England.'"[67]

Both Clare Boothe Luce and Millicent Rogers gave him expensive gifts. "Dahl had no qualms about laying claim to the perks of war and took to bragging about his many conquests to Creekmore Fath, who was convinced his friend was 'one of the biggest cocksmen in Washington.' Fath remembered Dahl proudly showing off various trinkets bestowed upon him by his various admirers as tokens of their affection. The most famous of these was Millicent Rogers, the Standard Oil heiress, …, who presented Dahl with a Tiffany gold key to her front door, along with a gold cigarette case and lighter."[68]

"Forty-one and freshly divorced when she met Dahl, she was independent and adventurous and inclined to similar men. Dahl found her intoxicating:

wide-set blue eyes, high cheekbones, and alabaster skin framed by soft shining hair in a pageboy cut. She was intelligent, with a quick wit and well-developed gift for mimicry that made her quite devastating at parties, and the best company. More than anything it was her forceful personality and originality that distinguished her from other society women. She dressed with enormous flair, in creations of the greatest couturiers of the day, from Mainbocher and Schiaparelli to Charles James, remaking their clothes to complement her long frame (5' 9") and pairing them with dramatic twenty-four-carat jewelry of her own design, so that no one who saw her would ever forget it. She favored attention-getting costumes, appearing one day as a Tyrolean peasant, in a dirndl and matching hat, and the next as Marie Antoinette, swathed in yards of silk taffeta."[69]

"Dahl had also been seeing rather a lot of Millicent Rogers, which was an occupation in itself. He had spent the Easter holidays at her estate in Virginia, and they had gone on a number of weekend getaways. She had been kind enough to invite him to stay with her while his Georgetown house was being redecorated, so he spent the latter part of the summer living in splendor. He was terribly impressed with her art collection, which he studied closely in his spare time."[70]

Arturo II remembers, "Dahl was ambitious, young, charming, and good looking. He was charismatic and able to recount humorous stories well. He had no personal or social connections of his own, and had to rely solely on his charisma and looks to seduce socially prominent and important American women. From the time he and Mother became lovers, he and I became truly great friends or, as the British would say, chums. When he screwed up in his relationship with Mother, he would call me and say, 'Let's have lunch.' And we would meet at a little French restaurant, Le Bistro. I would advise him to go to Bergdorf's and buy the sexiest sheer pair of French 'knickers,' along with one long stemmed red rose and two yellow roses. He was to send them all up to her apartment on 68th Street with the message, 'Oops, did it again. Dahl.' The next day I would receive a message at my office saying, 'A. P. – merci beau coups. R. D.'"[71]

"...Rogers lived in an eighteenth-century manor (Claremont) in Tidewater, Virginia, that more closely resembled a museum than a home. Dahl, who thanks to Millicent was fast developing a taste for the finer things in life, was bowled over by her collection of art, which included treasures from all over the world, including Empire and Biedermeier furniture rescued from her Arlberg chalet and a trove of modern French paintings. Inspired by her eclectic finds, from a group of antique clocks to a cluster of superb drawings by Watteau, Fragonard, and Boucher, Dahl vowed that as soon as he had enough put away, he would begin buying paintings for a modest collection of his own. Rogers' house was a jewel box, crammed full of furniture and objects she had picked up along the way from her marriages and many travels, but every piece told a story, and taken together they added up to something more and seemed to him evidence of a life well lived.

"Rogers rarely stayed in one place for long and flitted between several grand residences, including a sumptuous town house on Manhattan's East 68th Street. She spent much of her time in New York, where she chaired the Medical and Surgical Relief Committee.... Although earnest about her work, she had a delicate constitution and a short attention span. She had no interest in marrying again, but, spoiled and willful, demanded her lovers to be at her beck and call. It did not take long for Dahl to discover that she could be temperamental and controlling. She played musical chairs with men and seemed to have secret lovers tucked away in every European capital (throughout her life). An incorrigible flirt himself, Dahl was not particularly disturbed. He enjoyed being a part of her swell crowd and made the most of it."[72]

And, "In honor of Dahl's birthday that September (1944)–he turned twenty-eight on the thirteenth–Rogers threw him a fancy party and invited the usual cast of ambassadors, diplomats, undersecretaries of state, and assorted socialites and sycophants. Everyone sipped champagne and made polite chatter, and Dahl later complained that he found the whole thing a crashing bore."[73]

Dahl described his early life in two books, *Boy* and *Going Solo*. His parents were from Norway, but he was born in Wales on Sept 13, 1916. He went to prep and public schools, which were very cruel. He grew to 6'6" tall. When war broke out, he joined the RAF (Royal Air Force) in Nairobi. Dahl died in November 1990 at the age of 74 of a rare blood disease, myelodysplastic anaemia, sometimes called "pre-leukemia," in Oxford and was buried in the cemetery at the parish church of Saint Peter and Paul in Great Missenden. According to his granddaughter (Sophie, a model) the family gave him a "sort of Viking Funeral. He was buried with his snooker cues, some very good burgundy, chocolates, HB Pencils and a power saw."[74]

Arturo II adds a postscript about Dahl, "Months after Mother died he called me up and informed me that he wanted his painting back that he had given her and learned that I had it. I had purchased the semi-nude painting of a woman, by the artist Smith, from Mother's estate. His instant angry retort was, 'It's mine and I want it back!' The painting had no great commercial value and had he been civilized or a gentleman about it, I most probably would have given it back for what I had paid the estate for it. He brusquely informed me that if I did not GIVE it back to him, our friendship would be terminated. I never heard or saw him ever again."[75]

Dave Cordova. Smith painting given to Millicent by Roald Dahl. (Courtesy Arturo Peralta-Ramos II.)

Jamaica, 1945: Bond, James Bond, "Not much of Hoagy Carmichael there, thought Bond, as he filled a flat, light gun-metal box with fifty of the Morland cigarettes with the triple gold band." The quote from *Casino Royale* possibly refers to the Faberge gold cigarette case that Millicent gave to Ian Fleming during a stay in Jamaica. Her affair with Fleming was so intense, that Fleming, in an article about his days in Jamaica with Millicent, described her as having an insatiable sex drive.

Ian Fleming. (Courtesy *Life* Magazine.)

After the war ended, many of Millicent's friends in the intelligence world bought houses and wintered in Jamaica. This included William Wiseman, William Stephenson, Lord Beaverbrook, Ivar Bryce, Noel Coward, Perry Brownlow, and Ian Fleming. It was in late 1945, after his demobilization, that Fleming stopped in New

York on his way to Jamaica and entered into an affair with Millicent. They stayed for some time at Claremont Manor, and the affair may have been one of the reasons why, in 1945, Millicent purchased a house, Wharf House, across from Montego Bay.

"Others admired her double nature: she was a sensualist, but she thought like a man. 'She was so strong, but so feminine, so very female,' recalls Arturo Ramos (Arturo Peralta-Ramos II). 'And yet she demanded a brain out of the men in her life.' Of her known lovers, the most frequently mentioned is Ian Fleming.[76]

"Tommy and Oatsie Leiter had a house in Jamaica. The first time Oatsie met Ian she took him to task for his cavalier treatment of Millicent Rogers, who had joined the winter exodus to the sun. 'Mr. Fleming,' she said, when they were introduced, 'I consider you a cad.' 'You're quite right, Mrs. Leiter,' Ian replied. 'Shall we drink on it?'"[77]

Ian Fleming was a charmer and had a reputation for being nasty at times. He remained friends with Arturo II until his death. In all those years he never said a bad word about Millicent to Arturo.

Oatsie later introduced Fleming to John F. Kennedy. Tommy Leiter's name was used for the ongoing character of Felix Leiter in the Bond novels. Ivor Felix Bryce was another of Fleming's friends, and had been his roommate at Eton. Kennedy's positive comments on the novel introduced it to the American public, after which Fleming became wildly popular.

Ian Fleming was a journalist, and Second World War British Naval Commander. In 1939 Rear Admiral John Godfrey recruited Ian Fleming as his personal assistant with the code name 17F. Wikipedia states, "Fleming also formulated Operation Goldeneye, a plan to maintain communication with Gibraltar as well as a plan of defense in the unlikely event that Spain joined the Axis Powers and, together with Germany, invaded the Mediterranean colony." Later, when he built his Jamaican estate, he named it Golden Eye. While in Jamaica, Millicent sculpted a bust of Ian, which is still in the family.

Dave Cordova. Bust of Ian Fleming sculpted by Millicent. (Courtesy Arturo Peralta-Ramos II.)

"Dahl and Fleming had not gotten on well because of Ian's affair with Millicent Rogers, who was also a regular visitor to the island (Jamaica). Their dalliance had reportedly not ended well, and the two men had words over it. At the time, Fleming was carrying on a long, tortured affair with Lady Anne Rothermere, the wife of the *Daily Mail* proprietor Esmond Rothermere, and Dahl, probably out of envy as much as principle, was piqued by his caddish behavior. When Anne later became pregnant, however, Fleming stepped up and did 'the right thing.' ... Ian and Anne were married in Jamaica in March 1952. After a celebration at Golden Eye, complete with serenade by Noël Coward, they flew to Nassau, and then to New York, to be feted by the Bryces.

"By the time Dahl and Fleming met up again in New York, they had long since patched up their friendship."[78]

Millicent spent time with her close friend Diana Vreeland, editor of the fashion magazine *Harpers Bazaar* when Millicent knew her. They were in the same social circle and Diana used Millicent as a model. It could be called a friendship by haute couture, Diana Vreeland recalls, "Have I ever told you about the night I saw Millicent at a party at the old Ritz-Carlton here in New York? She started out the evening wearing a dress by Paquin–black silk with a bustle and a train. When a dessert was served, she spilled some ice cream and left the room to change into another dress. When coffee was served she spilled some of that and went off to change into another dress. Millicent's pure American: Standard Oil–that's H.H. Rogers. ... Millicent liked beautiful men, and she was just mad about Clark Gable. Mad! They were having a big love affair. He wasn't all that handsome. His head was too big. She was seductive beyond discipline...a lot for Clark to handle. Perhaps a European could have done it, but he was an American and he was very naïve. He was meat and potatoes–and sex. I'm sure he was never terrible to her in the way of cheating on her in a common way, but he drank. Clark would order three cases of scotch, lock himself in his hotel room, and give orders that no calls were to be put through. He didn't shave. He didn't bathe – he drank. And ten days later, or two weeks later he emerged."[79]

Diana Vreeland cites another incident. "Did you know I'm always having the most extraordinary conversations with taxicab drivers? They have a view, I can tell you, on everything. Just the other day I walked out to the corner of Park Avenue, hailed a cab, stepped into it, and asked to be taken to the (Metropolitan) Museum. … After five blocks or so, the cab stopped at a red light and the driver (Irving) said, 'Madam'–I knew he'd been looking at me in the mirror for the past five blocks–'would you mind if I asked you a question? Do you remember in the middle of the war when I drove you and Clark Gable to the end of Long Island to visit your friend Millicent Rogers?'

"'Yes,' I said, 'I remember it very well. And I remember you, too.'

"Millicent had picked up this driver during the war. Because of the gas rationing, she wasn't allowed a car and driver, but she took a fancy to this man and his taxi, and he practically became a member of the family. She'd send him out with her maid to match a pair of sandals, or if she needed her maid at home, she'd send him out to match this color shirt or this color cardigan. … Eventually, he became totally her employee, and anytime the two of us went anywhere, she'd send this taxi for me, and this man. Her one and only beloved taxi driver.

"He never looked around at me. He looked through the mirror and we talked about Millicent Rogers the rest of the way to the Museum."[80]

Clark Gable, circa 1934. (Courtesy Corbis Images.)

HOLLYWOOD

At about 12 years of age, Jackie Peralta-Ramos was an accomplished equestrian and rode regularly on favorite trails in the San Fernando Valley exercising horses for Clark Gable and others. One day she discovered stakes planted in the ground, thinking they were markers for a building foundation. She began pulling them up because they were in her prized horse trail, when she sensed people standing over her. She looked up and recognized Clark Gable with a beautiful woman, who turned out to be Millicent Rogers. Millicent was building a home on the site. Clark threatened Jackie, "I knew it was you. I'm going to spank your ass." Although somewhat embarrassed by being caught pulling up the stakes, Jackie remembers being struck by the beautiful seashell pin, from which a figure of a horse emerged, that Millicent was wearing on her jacket. Jackie thought that this must be a wonderful woman if she loved horses. That was the last time she pulled up stakes. Later Arturo II gave his mother's seashell pin with the horse to Jackie on one of their wedding anniversaries.

Millicent Rogers first met Clark Gable, popular actor and famed for his role as Rhett Butler in *Gone With the Wind*, at the parental home of Rocky Cooper in Southampton in 1942. Rocky Cooper was the wife of the actor Gary Cooper. It was the smitten Clark who persuaded Millicent to move to Hollywood in 1946.

"I do not believe," Arturo states, "that MR purchased Falcons Lair, the home of Rudolph Valentino, rather she rented it furnished with intentions of buying a house. She ordered her furniture sent out from New York. She became very unhappy after a short time (only about four or five months) in the house as she found it very eerie and morbidly depressing and definitely not a happy contented house."

Shortly after Valentino's sudden death, there were rumors about his ghost haunting Falcon Lair. People claimed to have seen him. A caretaker was said to have witnessed Valentino's apparition and ran screaming that he had seen him that night. It was whispered that a stableman left the estate and his job when he saw the actor petting his favorite horse. A woman friend was visiting and she heard footsteps and saw doors open and shut. She was in the mansion alone with Valentino's two favorite watchdogs, Brownie and Rudy. The dogs were good guard animals and trained to bark or growl at people, with the exception of Valentino. Their reaction was to whimper.[81]

"(Paul) Peralta-Ramos said his mother designed 'lots of jewelry in L.A.' during the summer of 1946 when she rented Falcon Lair. She always carried jeweler's tools and would work on designs on the train to California,' he added."[82]

Millicent had been designing custom jewelry since the 1930's. Millicent's friend, Alexander Schaffer of the antique Russian jewelry store in New York, A

La Vieille Russie, first helped her purchase Fabergé eggs, and then suggested that she start fabricating her own creations and introduced her to Joseph Fried, a metallurgist and jewelry maker. He taught her how to cast her own work, how to mix metals, and to set stones. Later, in Taos, she built a forge off her bedroom and spent many hours designing and creating her own jewelry.

Dorothy Brandenburg reiterated Millicent's jewelry making, saying that Millicent was always asking, "Where is my bludgeon?" meaning her tool bag. Dorothy Brandenburg was the daughter of the Taos artist Oscar Berninghaus, one of the Taos Society of Artists. Dorothy became one of Millicent's close Taos friends, along with Frieda Lawrence and Dorothy Brett. Millicent shared her love of jewelry making, teaching the art to Rocky Cooper and Benito Suazo from Taos Pueblo. Arturo adds, "I met with Maria Cooper, Gary's daughter, thinking she might have some of Millicent's jewelry. She didn't, but she said that Rocky continued to design and make her own jewelry thereafter."[83]

"She spent part of the early spring at Falcon Lair and with Clark Gable at his San Fernando Valley Ranch, when he wasn't working. Seeing how miserable she was at the Falcon Lair house, he proceeded to show her a very beautiful slightly rolling hillside property northeast of his ranch and above a small captivating damned lake. She fell immediately in love with the property and instantly arranged to purchase it. (Note: This is the property where Jackie as a teenage girl used to ride and exercise her own, Clark Gable's, and (Gilbert) Adrian's horses.)

"Once the purchase was accomplished MR, Gable, and the Coopers proceeded to go to Southampton where Rocky's stepfather Paul Shields, a long time great friend of both my father and MR, had his summer house. While in Southampton, Rocky kindly proceeded to locate a house very close to theirs in Beverly Hills belonging to her friend Annabella Power, Tyrone Power's recent ex-wife.

"In August 1946 MR, with Paulie (Paul Peralta-Ramos) and Clark, returned by train to Beverly Hills where she and Paulie happily moved into Annabella's house. While there Millicent was working with various architects for the building of her intended home in the hills of San Fernando Valley and happily being with and around Clark Gable. MR was never a party-goer, but suddenly she became a party-giver. She surrounded herself with numerous new friends of Clark Gable's and many of her old friends from the past like Claudette Colbert and her doctor husband, Dr. Joel Pressman, Reginald Gardner, Otto Lang (from Hannes Schneider's St. Anton's Alberg Famous Ski School), Gilbert Adrian and Janet Gaynor, Moira Shearer, Clifton Webb, Mrs. Norman Chandler (owned the *Los Angeles Times*), Oleg Casini, Hank and MR's cousin Frances Fonda, Jimmy and Gloria Stewart, Cole and Linda Porter, William and Bootsy Hearst, Prince and Princess Vitetti, Margaret Mallory, Van Truex, Diana Vreeland, William and Babe Paley, and the list went on and on."[84]

Arturo spoke of the time when Millicent jokingly told Yul Brynner that she never made the first act of a play and suggested they invert the acts so she could see the first one. With his usual heavy laughter, he replied, "Must tell the producer and director this so once a week we should do it so late arrivals don't disrupt our momentous dialogue at a critical moment stumbling in darkness down the aisles." Paul and Arturo were always on time, perhaps to compensate for their mother's tardiness.

Jimmy Stewart and Hank Fonda, whenever they were at Millicent's, managed to keep their friendship intact by agreeing never to discuss politics together as their political views were at opposite ends of the spectrum.

"At one of these parties Adrian arrived with a black and white small Gibbon monkey on his shoulder. Mother instantly fell in love with it. Three days later at a small lunch at Annabella's house Reginald Gardner arrived with an identical monkey on his shoulder. With great glee he presented to mother the monkey as a present. According to Van Truex, who recounted the story to MBR (Mary Benjamin Rogers), who later then told us about it, Reggie Gardner got a glass of champagne and taking the monkey off his shoulders, took a long sip from the glass and then let the monkey have a sip and then toasted mother with the following speech, 'May this new loveable pet give you as much pleasure, love and joy as Clark gives you!' Upon taking the monkey in her arms and taking a sip of champagne from Reggie's glass, turned to her guests and proclaimed, 'I shall name him Topaz and I'm confident he shall equal my friend Mr. Gable.' This in turn brought a great mirth of laughter to the group and they all toasted 'To Gable and Topaz!' Unfortunately, unbeknownst to most people, monkeys are prone to alcohol and poor Topaz, being the life of all her parties, died within a year of 'toasted' alcoholism."[85] Arturo reiterates about his mother, "It has been stated that Ayn Rand used her friend Millicent to depict her heroine in *The Fountainhead*. Gary and Rocky Cooper used to tease Mother about this when she became a little 'tough or stubborn.' Her heroine (Dominque) was then played phenomenally by Patricia Neal, Roald Dahl's wife!"[86]

Millicent, on many days when not feeling strong or well, spent the day in bed reading and translating previously untranslated books to English and had all her meals in bed. From her bedroom window she could look down and see the beautiful and well-manicured lawns of Annabella's house. There were hedges half sheltering the pool and pool house. One afternoon, she heard voices down at the pool, and looked out of her bedroom window. There was 14-year-old Paul at the pool with an older blonde woman trying to seduce him. Millicent dashed down to put a stop to it and saw it was Lana Turner, one of Clark Gable's former lovers.

Paul later related to his brother, "As MR approached, she slowly and deliberately looked both of us up and down for a few uncomfortable moments. She had icy composure, and spoke to Lana, 'Madam, God created man and to prevent his solitude and loneliness, he took a rib from him and created Eve. And, by God you are not Eve! Now, remove your nakedness and get out.' Turning to me, she said, 'I'll talk to you later.' She then calmly walked back to the house." Arturo added, "He never revealed what Mother had to say to him, other than ending the lecture with a sigh, saying, 'Oh well, I guess you are growing up sooner than I imagined. Most certainly learn to be a gentleman about the affair and do not brag about it to anyone.'"[87]

Arturo Peralta-Ramos wrote a note for the authors, "I only saw MR a couple of times during that time. She appeared deliriously happy with Clark and bubbled over with new vitality and strength, especially from the preparations to build the new house in San Fernando. Both appeared very content and extremely happy with each other.

"The cause of the breakup was a dinner party whereby Mother was to meet Gable after his day's shooting (on *The Hucksters*) was finished. The shooting ran late and Mother received a call from Clark saying they were running late and he would not make it to the dinner, but would call her the next day. Mother made some excuse, and went back to Annabella Power's house, which she had rented from her. Since it wasn't that late she packed up some Champagne, home-made bread, and a large can of 'Iranian Golden Caviar,' which she knew Clark loved. With that in hand she and the chauffeur proceeded over to the San Fernando Valley where Clark had his ranch. Seeing the lights out and having a key to the house, given to her by Clark, told the chauffeur to wait while she dropped off her little prepared basket of goodies.

"Knowing the house very well she turned on a small light and headed toward the kitchen. Ill-fatedly she heard a quite familiar sound coming from the bedroom and realized Clark was home and certainly not alone! Quietly entering the kitchen, she placed the Champagne, caviar, and bread into the icebox. Finding paper and pencil, she wrote out a very personalized note to Clark and taped it on the icebox door.

"The following is the only part I was ever specifically informed of by Clark of the contents within the note she wrote – 'Find cold bottle of Champagne/ your favorite caviar and home made bread in icebox for both you and your lady friend's breakfast. Please never call me again!' The lady was his long time girl friend Virginia Gray, a young and pretty actress! Later Mother did write a long very personalized letter later to Clark that his secretary probably typed out and turned over to Luella Parsons, (sic Louella Parsons), a society columnist. It was later claimed that mother sent this letter to Parsons personally. This was completely untrue as she informed both Paul and myself she had written Clark a long personalized letter of 'Good-by.' Mother *always handwrote* her letters."[88]

A partial quote from the farewell letter Millicent sent to Clark that was forwarded to Louella Parsons:

My darling Clark,

I want to thank you, my dear, for taking care of me last year, for the happiness and pleasure of the days and hours spent with you; for the kind, sweet things you have said to me and done for me in so many ways, none of which I shall forget. ... god bless you, most darling Darling. Be gentle with yourself. Allow yourself happiness. There is no paying life in advance for what it will do to you. It asks of one's unarmored heart, and one must give it. There is no other way. When you find happiness, take it. Don't question too much.

Goodbye, my Clark. I love you as I always shall.[89]

Soon after Arturo recalled talking to his mother about the breakup, "It was about 11:00 and she'd finished breakfast and was reading the morning paper. I came into her room and sat on the edge of the bed. We talked frivolously for a while, and then I decided to come right out and ask her, 'Why, when you were so in love with him, did you–of all people–react the way you did? I know you are not possessive or covetous of anyone or anything, and I know you are not a jealous human being. Please just tell me why?'

"She looked at me silently for quite a while. Finally she reached over to her bedside table, lit a cigarette, took a long drag, and exhaled the smoke. Her face did not reveal surprise, annoyance, or anger. A gentle ethereal smile emerged across her face, and then she replied, 'You know, Brother, I knew that sooner or later you would be the one to confront me regarding my actions or apparent behavior. Yes, I was and still am heartbroken by the loss of Clark, but remember I've had to live my days never being able to count on the certainty of another day. I learned early never to pity myself nor envy others for the things that were impossible for me to do. I've had many lovers in my life, and I gave without reservation all I could, each day. I was told that I should never have children, yet I had you three. A day to others was a lifetime to me. All normal and proud men love women and Clark was no exception to this. I love him for his intelligence, his bravado, his gentility, his lovely and thoughtful kindnesses towards others, and–believe it or not–his love of beautiful women and their attraction to him. Never once did he flaunt anyone or anything before me. Clark reminded me of three other men: your father, Ian Fleming, and Serge Obolensky. These three men left their mark of brightness, gentility, strength, and love on every woman they were ever with or bedded. They never make a woman feel inferior. I left Clark, not because I had a lack of love, nor because he was having an outside affair, but because he gave me the key to his home and when I discovered them there, it destroyed everything between us. That was that.' She sat up, reached for another cigarette, inhaled, and held the smoke in her lungs."[90]

In a memoir by Harry Furniss, he describes his cousin Mary who "…took on another unusual job. She was hired by the Rogers family (Standard Oil) to advise Teenage heir Count Peter Salm on his social responsibilities in handling the vast wealth he had inherited. The Count was the son of MR who at one point almost became Mrs. Clark Gable. …

"But about Clark Gable. The heiress (Millicent) and the actor planned to live on the West Coast. Feeling that perhaps Tinsel Town didn't offer quite the scale of luxury she enjoyed in her eastern domestic establishments, Millicent directed Cousin Mary to organize a truck convoy, forthwith, to:

pick up the silver from house A

" " " china " " B

" " " stoneware " " C

And the favorite carpets at D

And from everywhere clothes, bric-a-brac, a chef, servants, etc.

"All this Cousin Mary organized with her usual, calm efficiency. But no sooner was the cavalcade out of sight, heading west, than she received another directive: 'Wedding off. Returning to East Coast. Please return silver to A, china to B, etc.'

"After contacting the police in umpteen mid-west states, the convoy of trucks was located, and turned around. And they lived happily ever after, even Millicent without Clark."[91]

In 1932 (William) Faulkner went dove hunting with Howard Hawks and a friend of his, an actor named Clark Gable. Hawks began talking with Faulkner about books, during which Gable remained silent. Finally, Gable asked Faulkner who he thought were the best living writers. After a moment Faulkner answered, "Ernest Hemingway, Willa Cather, Thomas Mann, John dos Passos, and myself."

Gable paused for a moment and said, "Oh, do you write?"

"Yes, Mr. Gable," Faulkner said. "What do you do?"[92] In 1947, Arturo recalls this about his mother: "I had been in a serious car accident outside of Charlottesville, Virginia late on Friday, 23rd May. That Sunday MR, in California, and Paul in Connecticut, heard on the Walter Winchell's Sunday night broadcast that I had been killed in the previous night's accident. However, both my father and Peter had been called by the VA State Police late Saturday when it was discovered who I was, and that I was in the University of Virginia's Hospital, and still alive. They both in turn, after much confusion, pre-warned Mother and MBR (Mary Benjamin Rogers) that, though seriously injured, I was still alive. They immediately got together and drove down from Princeton, NJ, where Peter was in university, and they picked up my father near Doylestown, PA, where he lived and raced down to Charlottesville. Poor Paul, in school in Connecticut, heard from his floor's school master, John Joseph, of the Sunday's Winchell report and instantly, with Paul, located, and with intensely confused problems, contacted MR in California to notify her of my death. In exceedingly composed control, according to Paul, she informed him that they had been misinformed by the typical Winchell misleading report and that – 'Brother is still very much alive though badly damaged and unconscious. But darling Paulie, knowing "Brother," he will outlive us all. As soon as I am informed more about his condition, don't worry I will keep you well informed. Remember this, this isn't His First Close Call. Your father and Peter are down there with him.' That was the beginning of the great friendship and close relationship between MR, Paul, the family, and like Van Truex–John Joseph!

"One has to understand Mother's words or apparent coldness or indifference was far from reality. Rather having faced the possibility, within herself, of death every day and night, she saw death only as a moment at the end of time, and sadness was for those who lived thereafter.

"Near the end of June I left the hospital and went to Southampton. Knowing my uncle Henry Rogers III and wife Diana would be at their Southampton home, I went to see them since I was always close to the two of them. The family highly disapproved of the three of us seeing them because of their serious alcoholism. I always disobeyed and went to see them whenever I could; and I must say that neither ever drank in my presence, nor did I ever see either of them drunk! Henry was never a handsome man, rather undistinguished dirty-blondish hair with slightly heavy glasses and Diana was a non-bright woman with amusing charm and lovely lost-once figure even though one knew she matched him drink for drink. Henry to me was well-educated and a respected graduate of Oxford University. He was well-read, especially in Ancient World History and Science. Bright beyond words in inventive scientific electronics and in the physics dealing with matter and energy and their interactions in the fields of acoustics, magnetism and their retrospect to the physical properties and composition of things. Lamentably no one in the family, possibly other than Diana and me, knew he had numerous patents in his name; and he apparently had worked closely with, if I recall correctly, General Electric. Upon his death at 43, from sclerosis of the liver, when MR and MBR went to help Diana clean out his Hollywood house, they discovered a hidden room (referred to me once by Diana as your 'Uncle Henry's Playroom'). It was beneath the house and filled with hand-written papers, scientific books and magazines, and a mass of highly accumulated scientific equipment. Unfortuitously, neither MR, MBR, nor Diana knew what was in the clutter of disarray and all was dispersed to the garbage pile. Shortly after Henry was buried and the refuse disposed, General Electric contacted MBR and Diana asking if they could go through Henry's laboratory and files as he was working on a "Confidential Scientific Project" with them!!!!!!!!!"[93]

MILLICENT ROGERS

"THE MOUNTAINS HOLD ME IN TAOS"

Arturo Peralta-Ramos II wrote this chapter. He joined his mother in Taos a day after she first arrived. He reminisces:

"At some point in early August, 1947 the love affair with Clark Gable and Mother came to a sudden and gloomy end. All of Mother's old and newfound friends, both in California and New York, felt the same sadness for her. Adrian and Janet Gaynor, Gary and Rocky Cooper, Diana Vreeland and her son Tim, Henry and Frances Fonda, Claudette Colbert, Reggie Gardner, Clifton Webb, Cole and Linda Porter, and so many more tried to remedy the problem.

When Janet and Adrian realized they could not help heal the break-up of the affair between Clark and Mother, they were able to convince her to come and stay with them in New Mexico at their great sculptor friend Alan Clark's lovely western ranch near Santa Fe and there meet, if she so wished, numerous well-known writers, poets, and artists in the vicinity. Normally MR would have rejected this invitation, but she was never one to indulge in self-pity. Janet, Adrian, Claudette, and Rocky Cooper enticed to take her mind off the Gable situation by beguiling her incredible curiosity stating, that they would introduce her to the 'enlightenment' and 'enriched beauty' of the American southwest's various Indian tribal civilizations. Adrian seduced and captivated her inquisitiveness by informing her of the tribal Pueblo, Zuni, Hopi, Navajo, and Apache people and the creativity of their pottery, silver, weaving, basketry, and historical ancient dance, music, and cultural religious lore. They thought this would most likely enchant and captivate her artistic interests.

From what I gathered in conversation from Janet and Adrian, and was to hear and see personally later myself, was how Mother was to virtually instantaneously fall in love with the beauty and bounteous colors of the west when Janet and Adrian, Mother and her Claremont, sometime personal maid, cook and companion/friend, Ethel arrived in New Mexico. Ethel, whose father, Old Sam as he was known, had been a slave on the Claremont Manor Estate. He was born in 1864 or 1865, he never knew which. When MR brought the estate, part of the unanimous agreement by the sellers was that Old Sam would remain and be paid till the day he died. This agreement was kept by Mother!

Thus Janet and Adrian, Mother and Ethel boarded the Santa Fe Railroad from Los Angeles to Lamy, New Mexico, and thence traveled by car through the old Spanish city of Santa Fe. From there they drove for a number of miles north to the small adobe village of Pojoaque and its nearby Pojoaque Tribal Indian Pueblo. This tribal settlement nestled parallel to the Rio Grande River running north and south looked west upon the ancient high-rising rugged red mesas and the beauty of the Jemez Mountains. These mountains innocently guard the cryptic city of Los Alamos.

Once at Alan Clark's ranch, the party was invited to have lunch with Mabel Dodge Luhan in her home in Taos. This hostess was known for her literary and artistic salons in New York and New Mexico and continued to attract interesting and creative personages from all over. She had married Tony Lujan, a Taos Pueblo Indian.[94]

There was Tony in a white sheet, looking like a pope, and sitting in one of Mabel's Florentine chairs from Italy. He looked very pontifical and I was ready to bow and kiss his ring or something like that. 'Actually, he was a very sweet man,' Paul later said of him.

After Mother wrote Clark Gable that last letter, she changed. According to Adrian and Janet, 'She was like a child let loose in a toy store at Christmas. So far she's only seen Santa Clara's pottery, nearly every top Indian Trading Post, the American Indian Arts Museum, where she spent hours with the director and her new found friend Miranda Levy. She has bought various Navajo velvet blouses affixed with silver Indian buttons, skirts, and Indian low and high moccasins, which she now wears every day. She's bought up various rolls of velvet material to send to Charles James in New York to make up more blouses for herself and to inspire his collection. Miranda is helping her find old Indian silver buttons to go on them. She's already talking about staying on after we return to L.A.'

The following is in my words as recounted to me later by Mother in more detail, but reaffirmed by both Janet and Miranda in their earlier version to me:

The trip to Taos was done in an outlandish limousine that Adrian had rented in Santa Fe for the trip north on rather precarious roads. Leaving Alan Clark's ranch in Pojoaque at about 11:30 a.m., an hour very early and difficult for MR to make, Adrian driving with Mother at his side and Janet and Miranda in the back seat, they headed north through the little sleepy Spanish town of Espanola. Leaving Espanola, the Jemez Mountains receded to the west and the land around became dry and flat with only sagebrush and dry sand cluttered all about with small volcano-like mounds of prairie dogs warily sticking their heads out, while others ran back and forth between the sagebrush and small piñon before them. Roads boring straight for miles ahead, bumpy and filled with pot holes, which occasionally dipped without warning all over the place. Turning, MR looked back at Janet and with a wary smile on her face asked, 'I thought you said this was an easy, beautiful hour and a half drive to Taos?'

Adrian replied, 'Millicent, have I ever said to you something was completely different and utterly beautiful beyond words, that wasn't so?'

Coquettishly she instantly replied, 'Yes, my beloved Adrian, but this is a pot filled, bumpy dipping road, and not couture clothing!'

With great laughter from the back seat came, 'Touché!' and Adrian quietly drove on with a smile on his face.

As they passed the fruit valley of Velarde, they suddenly entered the enclosed Rio Grande Gorge road. At first the road paralleled the Rio Grande River on the left; and on the right the sudden sharp razor-like rocky canyon walls rose hundreds of feet above them. Suddenly MR became fully alive and fascinated with the narrowness of the river as the waters rushed by over small and large boulders, especially when she saw signs warning of 'watch for falling rocks, watch for land slides on road, slow twisting road.'

As the car entered the narrowing canyon, she became attentive to the sudden savagery of the rocky canyon wall on her side. Behind each blind curve they turned, the massive fallen rock slides climbed hundreds of feet straight up towards the sky above, while on her left the Rio Grande roared by over the numerous rocks, which had tumbled into it from her side. She noted that on her left and across the river appeared an ancient apparently abandoned roadway. Turning to Adrian, she asked why they had not kept on the roadway on that safer side.

As Adrian was much later to tell me, 'Your mother is instantly observant of things about her because her questions always are quite correct, though not always her facts.'

Miranda leaned forward and explained to her that that was the old abandoned Santa Fe to Alamosa, Colorado, narrow gauge railroad. The rails, engines, passenger and freight cars were all sold off in 1936 to Nationalist China. MR's only comment was to say it was a typical lack of imagination as it would have made an incredible tourist attraction journey. As they turned one sharp curve, ahead of them, in a cottonwood grove, appeared an ancient abandoned station and to its side the old wooden train water tower with its funneled water pipe still attached to the tower's side. Then suddenly, as they passed onto the next curve, leading left off their road, was the covered bridge crossing over the Rio Grande beneath and up and onto the station. Her comment as they rounded the next sharp curve was a disgruntled sigh and a 'Pity. Pity. Pity.'

As the car continued, she, with fascination, watched the disappearing train roadway as it commenced its long twisting climb up and out of sight of the river below and into far western mountains. As she relaxed back in the car contently looking at the majestic sight about her, her only comment was a despondent remark of, 'How could such a beautiful sight have been so wasted rather than utilized for its primitive, untouched beauty?'

For a time they drove on twisting and turning as they climbed out of the Rio Grande River Canyon. Suddenly a sharp and unexpected deep turn downward emerged leading into a very abrupt left and dangerously sharp horseshoe turn and upwards again onto an unforeseen and absolutely unexpected flat and far-out-reaching plateau.

Adrian pulled the car off the roadway and stopped near clumps of piñon trees. There before them was a sight so inconceivably beautiful that at first MR was speechless and absolutely stunned. According to Adrian, seeing MR absolutely mesmerized by the vision before her, he informed all to get out of the car. Janet, Adrian, and Miranda stood aside and watched Mother's astounded and overwhelmed face. Miranda laughingly later told me, 'Your mother looked like Lot's wife after she had illegally looked back at Sodom and Gomorrah and turned into a pillar of calcified salt!'

Finally, with still a mystified look on her face, MR turned to Janet and asked, 'Where has this been all my life? Why hasn't anyone ever told me about this place? I have traveled nearly all over the world and seen some of the most exhilarating panoramas that God has created for mankind, but never have I seen such an exalted nor spiritual setting as I see before me now.'

Spread out as far as she could see, lay the massive brown and black quarter-mile split in the open earthen plains, the split plunging straight down hundreds of massive rocky cliffs to the raging closely encased waters of the Rio Grande River running down from its headwaters in Colorado. Far to the left she could clearly see the San Juan forested mountain range and to the north and east before her the Sangre de Cristo Mountain Range, first seen and recorded for its majestic and magical spiritual beauty by the Spanish Conquistadors in the mid-sixteenth century.

Miranda told me how MR just stood there transfixed looking out beyond the pureness of the clear blue sky at the stark open prairie and slowly shook her head in apparent disbelief of what lay before her as though she was looking at and appraising a beautiful painting. Probably over ninety percent of people seeing this sight for the first time are absolutely taken aback by wonderment, awe, disbelief, reverence, puzzlement, excitement, spirituality and dozens of other expressive feelings and emotions. Much of it depends on the time of day and light, for each is different. Its enchantment and abounding beauty lies within each individual's self. When MR finally did turn around, she apparently had a very resplendent look upon her face. According to both Janet and Miranda, and also later, Adrian, it appeared as though she was only speaking to herself, as she stated,

'I think I now perceive and appreciate the descriptive Homer's narrative of the exploits and phe-nomenon described in his ancient Iliad on the voyages of Ulysses, as he stood on the bow of his ship and beheld the enigmatic wonders so spectacularly described. As I stand on this hill and look before me, I see the endless Great Wall of China built by Kublai Khan to keep his enemies out and here I see this incredible never endless, deepless gorged, inverted wall to do approximately the same.'

Miranda much later related to me, as she returned to the car, 'She politely apologized to all for holding everybody up, knowing Adrian had made reservations for some lovely place for lunch and thus didn't want to delay everyone any further. Adrian couldn't help silently laughing as he helped your Mother into the car, stating, "Millicent, Millicent my dear, please never, never change, you are truly unique and we all truly love you for it.'

Leaving the view area Adrian neared the little town of Ranchos de Taos and informed MR that they would be passing the famous second-oldest Spanish Catholic Church in the U.S. He explained to her that there is a stained glass window (it is actually a mystery painting) of Christ standing on the Holy Mound above the Sea of Galilee and that only at certain sunsets does He appear in the painting bearing His cross of crucifixion. Though MR was never a religious person per se, there were many individuals she read, such as Edgar Casey or Dr. Ryan of Duke University, who delved into mystical, unexplainable happenings or irrational situations, which left numerous questions in her mind, questions she would delve into for days, weeks, or months. Then later she would suddenly come up with extremely well-thought out prognostications of judgments or evaluation of potential predictions.

Adrian slowly circled the old adobe church and once again MR became absolutely absorbed in its mud adobe architecture with its strange beehive-like heavy buttresses, yet with its beautiful implicit primitivism. After circling the church, Miranda remembers her looking questioningly at Adrian and asking, 'If we have time before we leave, could we stop by so I can see the inside; plus I'd love to walk around and see its outer structure? I must say Vlaminck or van Gogh would have loved to have painted this church!'

Judith Bronner. Ranchos Church, Taos. (Courtesy Cliffshooter Photography.)

Miranda remembered being curious as to why it seemed so important for her, as a woman, to want to see the inside and just presumed it was the mysterious cross. Miranda said, 'Much later I was to realize it wasn't just to see the mysterious cross! Having just met her, I hadn't yet discovered her incredible inquisitiveness. Knowledge of architecture was part of that interest. I had known and heard of her impeccable style of design in clothing and jewelry, but I was to learn much about this beautiful woman's fascinating, sensuous, and erudite mind.'

Janet also later told me that the stronger and brighter men were, the more they adored and loved her or were unconsciously intimidated by her imperturbable equivalency. Diana Vreeland once told me, after Mother had died, 'Your mother unequivocally was one of the most, and I will use the word, Sexual Females I had the pleasure of ever knowing and loving! She was loved and adored by both men and women alike. She could walk into a crowded room and both men and woman looked and were captivated by her appearance and entrance. She was frightened of and always disdained any form of publicity. Yet without awareness, she created the very enigma of who she was.'

The film star Claudette Colbert, who also loved her dearly, once said to me about Mother, 'Movie stars are created by publicity, she is her own involuntary observed publicity.'

As they entered the Sagebrush Inn, she saw all the walls covered in magnificent old Indian weavings of blankets, floor rugs, and horse blankets. Her face exhibited the excited astonishment as she spun around, looking at all, exclaiming, 'My God, they're like magnificent French, Flemish, Italian, and Spanish tapestries of and for their own primitive idealistic culture. They're exquisite and stunning to the eye and the feelings that each exudes individually.'

Sedately, as usual, Adrian just smiled and replied, 'Millicent, we are late for lunch, so come along and you can look at them later, if we have time!'

Miranda laughingly was to tell me the above story much later because by then she had become accustomed to Mother's blithe innocence and the significance of seeing something new that captivated and excited her imagination. 'All during lunch she questioned Adrian, who gently pushed her off to me for the appropriate explanation to each question. Each question created a new, more detailed and pertinent question. Each question and answer made Adrian and Janet more fascinated and engrossed, until they were both as intrigued and asking as many questions as Millicent. The questions, such as Do all Indian tribes do this? When did they start weaving? Where did they get the looms, or did they make them? Who taught them? Where did they get the beautiful dyes for color? Since they were earth colors from the ground, who found these colors for them? Did all tribes have these colors near where they were?'

The main response, or answer that explained the color dye question became pertinent when Miranda explained that when the traders brought in the eastern German Town Blankets in the early 1800's for trade exchange, the Indians began trading for the white man's color pigments. This quickly led to the creation of the great variations in the Indians' weaving.

The conversation soon became a barrage of questions for Adrian with MR delving for the history of Indian tribal weaving. Janet wisely put a stop to poor Miranda's Indian Weaving Inquisition by informing them if Millicent were to see Taos and the Pueblo, they had better start right away before having to proceed to their friend Lieutenant Commander Richard Dicus' La Finca guest ranch close to the outskirts of Taos itself. According to Miranda, it was like schoolchildren being let out, with the scurry to get to the car and on!

Much later Mother was to tell Paul,

'Paulie, it was as if I was part of one of the people in Gulliver's Travels. A wide expanse of plain of desert and sage brush, various wild scattered clumps of desert flowers, small piñon trees dispersed like clusters of splattered paint across a canvas and surrounded in the far distance by brown and yellowish hills of pine and aspen. Centered directly in front of a metaphysical towering 13,000-foot mountain, lording it over all. It was an outrageous Remington or Berninghaus painted to thrill the eyes of bewildered eastern pilgrim wagon train settlers' first coming to the West. I am thrilled Paulie, for I have met one of the great American Western artists, Oscar Berninghaus, who I believe will become as famously recognized as Winslow Homer is to the East.'

Long after I had met the Honorable Dorothy Brett, I asked her if Mother had ever recounted her arrival to Taos with the Adrians, and her reply made me roar with laughter, but not surprise. 'Yes your mother was Alice in Wonderland looking through the glass!'

Brett informed me that at first Mother was disillusioned after their lunch at the Sagebrush because as they neared town, all beauty suddenly disappeared and nothing but run-down motels, third-hand cafes, garages, and bars emerged. Then unexpected, as though within a dream, an umbrella alley of beautiful tall and full cottonwood trees covered the sky from the pot-holed road. To the right a large grove of a variety of tall trees appeared, followed by an old lumberyard. To the left a long antiquated, two-storied, old wood icehouse from the early 1900's, followed immediately by a rather large food store attached to a Spanish-type old dance hall.

Then abruptly, at a small crossroad, the road narrowed and commenced to climb a narrow hill. Surprisingly, to the right appeared a lovely old late-eighteen-hundreds Victorian Gingerbread house perched on a slightly higher hill than the road itself. Janet, having been to Taos on numerous occasions both with Adrian and Miranda insightfully, awaited Millicent's forthcoming reactions on her entrance to Taos itself.

As they were to describe the event to me later, 'Directly ahead of us, on the right was a small two-iron-barred-windowed adobe building with typical overhead opened wood portal with a much used planked, gray walkway, hitching post railings and overhead a traditional wooden triangular signboard upon its parapet declaring U.S. Post Office.'

Janet clearly, laughingly, remembered Mother's comment at the time, 'I guess people don't get too much mail around here as no more than four people could possible get into that building without fully stepping froggy-style upon each other.'

As they slowly traversed up the narrowing roadway, on both sides appeared tightly attached adobe mud-walled buildings. Those on the left were apparently the backs of buildings facing the opposite direction. On the right a succession of one-story antiquated and mud-cracked adobe buildings of which repair had long been neglected and forgotten. Some store fronts were sealed with long-time sun-bleached boards as was the narrow boarded step-up or step-down walkway. Those still in business housed a variety of typical western merchandise: boots, bridles, and saddles; a tiny local barbershop with its old red and white candy bar-like sign still slowly rotating; a small heavily dust-covered liquor store; a western cowboy hats and jeans store, followed by a rather grubby appearing Lebanese food store; and finally a tightly squeezed-in gun and ammo store.

They reached the crest of the hill and the roadway opened to another four-way crossing. To the right set far back, far off the road in a clump of tall cottonwoods was another old, beautiful Victorian house. But to Mother's shock a mass of people suddenly appeared as if from nowhere. 'Your mother, in her typical forthright fashion, sat forward and looking at the mass before her stated, "Christ, what in Holy Hell is going on? Where did all these people appear from?"'

Adrian's, Miranda's, and Brett's renditions are pretty much identical. They explained that the greater mass of people, in various stages of western fashion, were amassed because this was the opening of San Geronimo Fiesta combined with the following day's Taos Indian Pueblo's ceremonies, for which people come from all over to see and be a part of.

Mother's version was pretty much as follows:

'When we reached what I thought was the center of town, I had the strangest feeling I had stepped back in time and that I was no longer in the Twentieth Century. On all the surrounding buildings' parapets were small. brown paper shopping bags placed two to three feet apart and filled with sand to keep them in place, and within them burned candles known as Luminarios. Even with the afternoon light, one could see the bright illuminating flame flickering, like little dancing fairies, ever so brightly inside. All about me were dozens of people in gaily colored costumes. The Spanish men had sombreros upon their heads, some with beards or semi-handle bar moustaches, *white shirts with leather vests, Spanish dark trousers with silver buttons running down their sides and various colored cowboy boots. They walked proudly and gallantly around. Spanish ladies of all ages had their abundant black hair combed stylishly back and held in place by enchanting large turtle shell or silver combs. Some had on white peasant blouses and others had variously colored open necked blouses with puffy short sleeves, exposing their rather large and round fleshy bosoms framing beautiful turquoise stone necklaces. Their long Flemish styled red or black skirts swished as they walked in high-heeled shoes to match. Young children were gleefully either eating mustard dripping hot dogs or fuzzy colored sticky cotton candy. They were dressed either as Indian chiefs carrying tomahawks or cowboys in shorts with pistols around their skinny waists. Amongst the numbers of people moving about were numerous older, very dignified Indians moving within the mass of the crowd. A few were reeling. What amazed and excited me the most were the older and most awe-inspiring dignified Indians with their colorful ceremonial blankets wound tightly around their waists and others draped ritualistically and loosely over their heads, their thick black braided pig-tailed hair descending like a spiritual aura over each shoulder. Their faces were marked and etched with long times gone, yet still proudly seen within their darkened, ageless eyes. I felt my heart and soul go out to them and wistfully wondered how I could help these proud overlooked and isolated people. I suddenly felt I knew that I had to know more about them before I could know how to help them and before they themselves lost their own sublime identity.*

Abruptly I was back again as I looked out at the rugged looking young cowboys with weathered faces and skin tight jeans, old cut-up worn boots, some with colored kerchiefs knotted tightly around their neck, and straw hats upon their young toughened, weathered faces. Tourists attempted to emulate the cowboys, unfortunately with their bellies hung over their new Concho silver belts and leather bolo ties. Their wives were in white off-the-shoulder blouses loaded under the weight of rather poor, though in rare cases superb, old turquoise necklaces. They were dancing Mexican Paso Doble dances in wildly colored ruffled Spanish/Mexican skirts within the tree-lined square.

'My thoughts were interrupted suddenly by a rather heavy-set, needing a shave, Mexican Deputy Sheriff in a short-sleeved khaki shirt with a large silver star on his barreled chest, heavy black leather belt with a holster hanging from his hip. He informed Adrian that he was not permitted to stop on the crossroad, and to move ahead or turn down the right hand road. As we turned, Adrian told me to quickly look down left into the town's square and see if I could see the old children's carousel. Unfortunately, I couldn't and he explained that right here was the oldest part of Taos with the frontier street exactly as it originally was. He also stated he would tell me the story of the merry-go-round later.'

Within the square is the La Fonda Hotel run then by a charming Greek family, the eldest John Karavas, a stagecoach shotgun rider from up in Silverton, Colorado, his brother Jim, and his wife Nouli, a short Greek gypsy-dressed queen of the roost. They ran the hotel with their son Saki, a handsome Greek, amusing, well-educated Lothario. The walls are covered in magnificent old Indian blankets and local art including pots and Kachinas.

The party turned right (down Kit Carson Road). As they traversed very slowly down the street it appeared like an old western Hollywood set. Nearly all the buildings on either side of the street were neglected mud-plastered adobe with their original frontage of old graying wood sidewalks and horse hitching post railings. Janet explained, 'The first building on the left is Sewell's Trading Post, one of the oldest and best for over-all mixed

Indian tribal artifacts of rugs and blankets, beaded Indian costumes, feathered headdresses, weaponry, primitive Katchinas, and old belts with silver concho buckles.

'Right next door is Kit Carson's home, pretty much furnished as it was, stark and spartan. Directly across the street in a kind of U, set in amongst the bushes and trees is La Dona Luz, considered one of the top restaurants and wine cellars in the U.S., though the proprietor is extremely arduous to deal with, but people still come up from Santa Fe just to have a dinner here. However the original owners, Ralph Meyers and Rowena, of the El Rincon Trading Post, which is another of the great old Indian trading posts, dating back to about 1890, lease the restaurant out. She's a delight and very knowledgeable about many old original tales of Taos and the West. Many of the same type of things are here as across the street, except there is a much larger collection of old Navajo and Zuni weavings. All the rest of the buildings are art galleries and more touristy type stores. There is one more very good old Indian store in the main square called Don Fernando, which is more into diverse Indian and Mexican primal silver, but also with numerous exceptional Indian woven blankets and rugs.'

As the car reached the end of the street another elderly Victorian building appeared, yet its appearance showed its gingerbread façade had been sorrowfully removed. Mother's immediate remark was both a question and a statement, 'How many of these wonderful reminiscent Victorian houses still remain in Taos; and does the town have a building ordinance that they cannot be torn down? Because, if not, like the narrow gauge in the gorge, Taos will be losing a big part of its past architectural history and major tourist revenue from those who would flock to see the assertive influence of Spanish, Mexican, Territorial, and Indian harmonious integration.'

Adrian's immediate retort, according to Miranda, was, 'Millicent you're an exalted, fantasizing dreamer and a remarkable envisioner of what could be, but unfortunately, rarely will be!"'

Without hesitation she retorted back, 'Queen Isabella accepted the impossible dream, and Columbus substantiated it. So there! Now tell me about the merry-go-round story.'

Supposedly, in good nature or politeness, Adrian asked Millicent if she had ever read D. H. Lawrence's short story, "The Rocking Horse Winner." After her affirmative reply, he told her that years before, in 1925, when Lawrence and Frieda were in Taos staying with Mabel Dodge Luhan, he had gone into town to see one of their fiestas and came upon the children's merry-go-round called the Tio Vivo. Being British and having seen carousels both in Britain and in France, he visualized the most elaborately detailed and intricate ones. But he was astounded and transfixed by the one he stood before in Taos. It was not the standard moveable up and down and around that captivated him. It was the actual individual horse carved figures themselves that captured his immediate attention. Each breathtakingly carved horse was distinctively and explicitly diverse in its active running positions and movement. Every individual horse's coat was of different coloration as though part of a wild prairie herd. Each head exemplified the slight wildness of fear in its eyes and the untamed freedom of its surroundings. No two legs of any horse matched the identical position movement of any other's stance as each was meticulously posed and carved in different running variations and positions to the other.

What apparently confounded Lawrence was the mechanics that made each of the horses appear to leap upward and forward in one motion and in the next appear to be back on the ground before their repeated forward leap. Yet no two horses appeared to neither rise at the same instance nor descend at the identical same time! The instant the Tio Vivo stopped, he worked his way through the mass of children waiting to buy a ticket and approached the old man who was running it and who spoke no English. Lawrence became obsessed with wanting to know more about the origin and creation of the mustang horses. According to Frieda Lawrence, wife of D.H. Lawrence, who still lived in Taos, he asked Mabel Luhan to find him a good interpreter, which she arranged for the following day. Bright and early he and his interpreter walked to the Plaza and met the old owner who was greasing and preparing the machinery for the day's business.

When I'd gotten to know Frieda many months later, I confronted her on the subject. She recalled and confirmed the Tio Vivo incident. However, because of long lapses in time she could not recollect much of the personal details regarding the background of the Tio Vivo other than she thought the owner or his brother had been either the German carpenter and the other a clock maker, or vice versa, who had both migrated to the U.S. some time in the early 1900's via Mexico. Frieda, in her usual deep heavy reverberating laughter and with great mirth asked, 'Vot ist it between you and your mutter that ist so interesting in dat story?'

I explained to her that Adrian had related the story to Mother when she first arrived in Taos and then she saw the Tio Vivo and also, like Lawrence, had become fascinated by the incredible sculptured carving of the horses' bodies and heads. Similar to Lawrence she also became especially enthralled by the hypnotizing effect of their bewitching faces, the fascinating mechanical workings. She felt it should be purchased and given to a major museum before they could become lost, separated, or destroyed. She had discreetly offered to purchase the entire Tio Vivo, but the offer was lamentably declined. She then attempted to have an artist do an oil or watercolor painting portraying the full-bodied mustang horse surrounded by four of the various free untamed heads. Unfortunately she could not find an artist who would or could truly sense and create the mythical feeling and grandeur she wanted and felt.[95]

Mother listened to the story with great intensity till Adrian suddenly had to turn off to the right onto a bumpy, dirt road leading into a small adobe-structured hamlet. As he drove slowly up the gutted road, he pointed out a small chapel and explained that the area was called Canyon and was still very much a Hispanic residential area. Pointing out the small chapel, still with its old cast iron bell in the antiquated roofed steeple, he explained that it was still an illegally practicing Penitente Morada of which there were numerous spread around Taos. In fact he stated that this one was very close to Mabel Luhan's hacienda. Instantly MR became intrigued and interested as to what it all meant. They continued driving in and around small neatly kept adobe houses, with fresh laundry hanging out on rope lines to dry, chickens, roosters, and ducks scattered about with small pigs and quite a few shaggy Heinz-57 variety mongrel dogs lazily sleeping or running about as the car passed by on the dust-covered areas around the houses.

Typically MR's observance, because of her love of animals, was, 'Well at least they seem well-fed. Now tell me more about this Penitente religion. Is or was this the old Charles V Flemish/Spanish 1450's Catholic religion, and if so did the Spanish Conquistadors bring it up from Mexico with them?'

According to Miranda, all three broke up laughing and Janet asked her, 'Millicent you're once again too much! You ask a relevant question, and then before someone has time to think it out, you answer your own question with complete comprehensive historical facts! The answer is most probably a resounding YES! But the person who can most likely give you its chronology is Richard Dicus as he loves all forms of history.'

With that response the car suddenly dipped down, through, and up over a rather steep semi-active arroyo. A few yards further on the mud-ditched road, the car entered the square building of the Dicus ranch. After introductions, confusing transfer of luggage to various rooms, congenial cocktails, and a very gratifying early dinner the long Saturday ended.

Since Mother was late to get moving in the mornings because of her disabilities, also in acclimatizing herself to the 7,000 foot altitude, the others had gone into town, the next morning, to see the local San Geronimo town fiesta and returned in time to pick Mother up for the invitational lunch at Mabel Luhan's."

Arturo adds greater detail to his mother's arrival in Taos:

"*The following day (after arriving at the Dicus hacienda) there was be a Taos Pueblo Indian Ceremonial Dance, which they visited. The Gaynors arranged with another old friend Mabel Dodge Luhan and her Taos Indian husband Tony Lujan, a former chieftain of the Taos Pueblo(Taos Pueblo does not have chiefs. The leaders are called. Governors. It is not established that Tony was a Governor, though he was well known for his drumming), to give a small buffet luncheon for well known international Taos artists–Oscar Berninghouse, Earnest Blumenschein, Honorable Dorothy Brett, daughter of Reginald Baliol Brett, the 2nd Viscount Esher, KCB, Leon Gaspar, and numerous others of the artist group. I will name just a few of the writers and MR's future friends: Victor Higgins, Ford Ruthling, Frank Waters, Saki Karavas, Victor White, and Frieda Lawrence, widow of D. H. Lawrence and supposed sister or cousin of the German WWI flying ace Baron Manfred von Richthofen (the Red Baron) and Frieda's long-time companion Angelino (Angelo Ravagli falsely rumored to have been the model for the lover of D.H. Lawrence's infamous Lady Chatterley's Lover). Rumor or not, Paul's and my opinion was that Angelino was a charming and typically entertaining Italian rogue, but a wonderful, kind and thoughtful friend and companion for Frieda. Because Mother spoke fluent Italian, German, Latin, and French, and was an occasional rascal herself, she became an instant friend (of Frieda's), and sometimes on casual close trips, a companion of Mother's till the day Mother died.*"

LIFE IN TAOS

When Millicent returned to Taos the next year, in 1948, to take up residence in a hotel while overseeing the building of her adobe home, her arrival into the little village of Taos was noted, if not on the society page, then by inhabitants who still chuckle over the furor.

Millicent took to the terrain like a scout and, with Paul driving her they traveled to the outlying pueblos, viewed ceremonial dances, and purchased Indian blankets and jewelry. On the Navajo reservation she chose the best of the woolen blankets. She acquired a collection of Indian and Hispanic artifacts that would be impossible to match today.

She began working for Indian rights with Frank Waters, author of the American classic *The Man Who Killed the Deer*. This was for the aid and political help of the southwestern Indian tribes. She became dedicated to this and other causes, such as she did during World War II when she raised more than $1 million for medical supplies to go to Europe and Asia.

When the Federal government closed the Pueblo Health Clinic, Millicent silently gave money to run it until the Government funded it again. She financed the trip to Washington, D.C., to protest the closing of the Clinic. Lucius Beebe, Frank Waters, Oliver La Farge, Tony Reyna, Tony Mirabal, Lupe Martinez, and Cruz Trujillo were part of this successful effort and journey.

She made friends with Tony Reyna, one of the most respected members of Taos Pueblo and proprietor of an Indian arts shop. "She appeared cool and aloof but in reality she was warm and friendly," Reyna says. "What I admired most in her was her great sense of appreciation."[96]

Millicent wrote a letter in August 1948 to John Joseph about her first impressions of New Mexico:

"Oh John,..... we are sorry (you are not here) because so many strange and exciting and beautiful things have been happening to us that we wished you had been with us in sharing..... also very funny things which I shall now try to tell.

"Yesterday we came back from Apache country where we spent two Winslow-Homer-Remington days of wild joy..... Madam (Mabel Dodge Luhan) of course tried to deter me .....

"My friend Margret Mallory arrived, we met her at San Juan Pueblo where Tony (Lujan) and seven Indians picked us up, from where we followed into beautiful wild country. Paul and Mr. Dicus (Commander Richard Dicus, owner of a Taos Guest Ranch where we stayed) having shoved off in the pick-up truck with Trinidad (one of the lead dancers of Taos Pueblo and the Indian who painted frescos for D. H. Lawrence and for Millicent Rogers), his wife, his brother George and wife, and Papa Joe.

"After about five hours of Tony-slow driving we arrived at Stinking Lake (one of the lakes at Dulce, N.M.), which is not really its name, to find that we were on a low hill among a mess of other tents and teepees all occupied by Indians. There Tony left us to go himself into another personal encampment; 'Don't like so many people of family, you don't mind?'

"From our hill we looked down over the small lake and many tents and teepees, all with their own small fires curling gently into still air.

"The two Kivas were of cut Aspens very green and cool. All around were sheep and goats and horses, some tethered some free. Young men and boys were racing up the slopes around, some bringing in the horses they were to race that evening….. which alas they did not do for some reason best known to themselves. Old women were cooking dinner for their families, children in bright colours were racing up and down, nameless drums were beating and from all over the camp the voices of men singing. It was like the pictures which one always longs to be in. AND THERE WE WERE IN IT.

"Later we went down to the Round Dance. Many people going as the name described in a circle, close together in a huddle with the drum in the middle with three men playing it. Everything in beat and everyone singing. You might expect it, and it was true, in the center was Tony singing as hard as his throat would allow him. Beating the drum and having a most excellent time. We danced around up a ditch and through a puddle and round back onto the flat, the circle getting bigger and bigger ….. hypnotic and great fun. I couldn't stop, I loved it madly!

"After a while the others all got tired so they insisted on going back to our camp. Joe, the old man fell in love with one of my blankets and asked if he could wear it so he took it to the dance and felt very happy with himself. Very sweet he was, and warm or so I thought, but the night air came down and since it became suddenly desperately cold all the fine coloured blankets which I had taken, frankly out of pure swank and for the pleasure of reds and blues, came into their own with a vengeance ….. Later when they found that we liked them men came who were cold and slept in our station wagon and around our fire and we covered as best we could.

"We made a fine warm soup of steak bone and gumbo and

peas which with the coffee we had ready and so anyone who had no place to go came to us. Strange how soon people find when they are welcome and these came gladly. Strange how few people know how to care for themselves.

"By the next day we seemed to know everyone and everyone seemed to know us, women came into the tent and looked at us and chatted and laughed, the very young children and papooses on their mother's backs, dogs and cats….. they all came and ate and drank with us and John all had good manners and all were clean.

"In the afternoon there was an ancient Indian foot race. Two sides, North and South. We Taos were North with Tony as the Head waving the runners on with the Aspen leafed switches; the old men in wonderfully beaded waistcoats on which were eagles and poppies and blue stripes and yellow shells embroidered. Our side won. The two sides divided. Then came the most extraordinary sight. One on either end of the runway. Each with its flag, ours red. They formed two groups, at the head of each walked the leader, with women dancing just behind them, the drums beat and they both sang advancing slowly toward each other. It had a ceremony suddenly.

"Behind our group came three lines of women on horseback, the center head of which was a magnificent and stately woman in red, as the groups met the head woman of the losing team advanced on foot and roundly insulted the Red woman who sat like one might imagine Bodesia (Boudica, Warrior Queen[97]) might have sat her horse and looked down. Then a woman on the side also on horse took from a box bunches of grapes and tossed them to the winners. Threw them at Tony. Tony wasn't Mabel's Indian, he was a great chief and he walked like royalty with ease and dignity, slowly and with power. It was a fine (image)…

"In the evening we had our own songs and finally a Round Dance on our hilltop. A little one. The big one on the plain below lasted all night and was going in the morning at seven when we got

up; It looked very funny, a little huddle of people in blankets going around in a circle in the early morning sun with the fires sent long quivers of blue smoke up into the air.

"In Rome, in Paris, in the East I have seen strange lovely things that excited and delighted me, but never, never anything which reached down inside and belonged to me as that camp did through every minute of the time spent there. It was America, into the center and core and it was personally mine in a most curious, easy at home way."[98]

According to John Joseph, this first encounter (with Taos) affected Rogers so strongly that she soon decided to look for a place to live. He wrote, "A bit of wind, a thin murmur, stirred the sage; a bird called plaintively; curls of smoke rose from Taos chimneys, some ten miles away the Sacred Mountain kept changing its colors in such a way as to make the mountain seem to be moving. She asked me if I hadn't felt that the mountain seemed to have a kind of motion, drawing near to us, then receding, almost, as she put it. 'beckoning' …and the last chapter of her life, in many ways was the grandest chapter of a grand life, the Taos chapter, had its beginning."[99]

Brett relates, "The following summer Rogers returned to Taos, rented a house (The Tony House, Tony Lujan's house on the Pueblo), and began searching for a place to buy. Succumbing to Mabel's 'advice and maneuvering,' she bought an old four-room adobe fronted by pastureland with a view of Taos Mountain."

The property, which she named Turtle Walk, is on Lower Ranchitos just as it meets Cottam Road. She bought the land from Judge Kiker.

Millicent and Freida Lawrence (widow of D. H. Lawrence) in front of the Tony House. (Courtesy Arturo Peralta-Ramos II.)

Turtle Walk, like all of Millicent's homes, was a canvas that she created. Millicent had models made of her homes as a decorating tool. Arturo still owns the model Millicent made of Turtle Walk.[100]

Millicent dove into the remodeling of her new Taos home. She enlisted the help of Brett and Trinidad Archuleta. Trinidad painted the frescos in the courtyard. He also painted the buffalo mural for D. H. Lawrence

Arturo Peralta-Ramos II. Aerial view of Turtle Walk taken from Arturo's plane. (Courtesy Arturo Peralta-Ramos II.)

on the side of his mountain ranch home. Brett painted designs on the vigas and ceilings and helped Millicent mix earth colors from local mud and dyes.

Dorothy Brett wrote about helping Millicent decorate Turtle Walk:

"Slowly through the summer the building went on, Millicent in a dream, with no plans drawn, would find that what she had in mind did not always work out the way she expected. Walls would go up; walls would come down; windows would be put in, taken out and put somewhere else. There was so much shifting and changing that we, the spectators, began to wonder whether a whole house would ever materialize. The patience of the builder and the friends working for her was strained to the breaking point, yet somehow or other a definite share rose out of the turmoil. Her bedroom, very high with a huge window, the width of the north wall, was the first room to be ready for painting. There followed the little turtle room several steps

Trinidad Archuleta. Bird fresco in Turtle Walk.
(Courtesy Arturo Peralta-Ramos III.)

down from her bedroom, which led into a guest room, and on down into the library, another large room.

At this period, I was called in to help with the painting of the walls. In the middle of the floor was assembled huge tins of paint, paints of many rich colours. Sitting on the floor Millicent would carefully mix and mix the colours until she got what she wanted. Her hands a mass of the whirl of paints she would mix patiently until she was sure of the colour and tone. Our headache was matching these later on as needless to say the amount was never sufficient. Harry the chauffeur and Trinidad climbed the ladders for the actual painting. Two walls of her bedroom were a rich Indian red, the third a lovely yellow. The heavy vigas a dark off shade of blue. From room to room we went, our scores of pots of paint following us. For weeks we lived surrounded by tins. We mixed and mixed, dripping paint on ourselves and moaning over the complexity of matching shades of colour. It was difficult. It would look alright in the pot; on the wall it would look a shade off. Millicent had a wonderful eye for colour... She had a very exact eye for tone... I would make notes of the colours used for certain shades, the amount, yet even so, on the wall, with a different cast of light, the tone would be too bright or too flat. What a chore it was, but also what fun!

...The flat roofs of adobe houses are our chief headaches. She had layers and layers of roofing paper put down... Furniture kept arriving from the East. With the Yaples she would drive all over the country looking for old windows, old doors, and so on. The pattern of the house formed a square. Inside this square was a patio and garden. The walls of the patio have weird animals painted on them, the vigas had Indian designs. The patio has a strange oriental quality, hard to define, due possibly to the old doors, the latticed windows, and the painted designs.

As the building and remodeling continued, Millicent gave one or two parties, one in the narrow old hall of the house, where the Indians managed somehow to dance, then an out door party in the Patio. It was then that Millicent's innocence of Taos and of the Indians was shown. The patio, which was at that time but a yard with mounds of dirt and was decorated with branches of cotton wood trees. They were stuck in the earth and looked surprising real and pretty. A big fire was built! Long wooden tables held the drinks and food. Under the table and alongside, crates held bottles, from Coka cola (sic) to whiskey, and therein lay her error. The party was scheduled for six. The guests began to assemble. Still no Millicent. Enormous pots of food began to arrive from the Fonda Hotel. Two bus loads of Indians arrived, then finally Millicent, looking lovely and bewildered. The party started in full swing. Some of the guests were already tight, were ill mannered enough to complain of the food and drink, which they imbibed quite freely, and stomped off in a huff. Meanwhile darkness fell and in the dark the wily Indians filched drink from the crates and nearly all of them became hopelessly drunk. The party in the firelight, among the false trees, assumed a joviality that became completely out of control. The Indians in their feathers and bells staggered around unable to dance. Some of the guests were also staggering around. Millicent was reduced to hopeless giggles. Then the party began to break up. Everyone concentrated, as much as they could concentrate, on coaxing the Indians back into the bus. Everybody seemed to be chasing Indians. At last they were shut firmly and safely into the bus and driven back to the Pueblo. Millicent, helpless and amused, learned her lesson and in so far as she was able the whisky was hidden at future parties.

She was faced with the problem we have all faced, which was the help! The most difficult of all was a cook. For a long time she had Pafalita (sic Crucita) and Isabel, nieces of Tony Lujan. These sisters cooked for her for many, many months. In the last few years she brought her old and trusted friend Ethel from Virginia, a marvelous cook. With her came two more coloured girls from Virginia, to look after the cleaning. Finally she was thoroughly established, the painting and planning of gardens and guests houses and servants' quarters went steadily on.

...She would drift into our houses with a gentle swish of skirts, and a low call. Frieda's cheery answer would boom out, and lunch or tea or supper would be laid ceremoniously in the dining room. Then there came a day when Frieda decided that Millicent had become an intimate friend, and she was promoted to eating in the kitchen; perhaps of all places the most delightful for eating in. Millicent accepted this change joyfully and became a constant informal guest. There was never any knowing when she would appear, but we were all certain that when she did, she would enjoy the unconventional meals in the kitchen as much as any of us. Frieda busy of the stove, Angy away off in the pottery, waiting for my call when lunch was ready, Millicent sitting at the table, telling her latest adventures of searching for old doors and windows, jewelry and Santos. What fun it was, and how lovely she looked in her wide skirts, velvet Navajo tunic, and lightly woven shawl! She loved shawls, She loved jewelry, until criticism made her shy of it. How much fun she had with all of us!

...I would be lying asleep on my sofa, and when I would feel someone tugging at my toes (Brett was deaf and had to rely on seeing her dog barking or someone tapping her to know there were guests.) and I would open a resentful eye, and there would be Millicent smiling at me. She would come to see of I were doing anything exciting in the way of painting. She bought my "Buffalo Dance," the "Turtle Dance," and many other paintings of mine. Some I gave to her as I have nothing to give except my paintings, and she gave me so much. One of her great gifts to me were the camping trips and the final marvelous trip to Jamaica.

The first trip I took with her was to Gallup.... We arrived very late at the El Rancho Hotel, rushed to the evening performance in the stadium, and again fell under the Indian spell. Millicent was enthralled. The masses of Indians of all tribes.... Millicent has walked into a fantastic world, to which her heart and soul belonged. She was in her spirit, in her way of life, a part of this world, far more so than that other world of perfect clothes social standing, and far too much money. Among the Indians she was at home; she was unknown, free, a human being among human beings....

Back at the hotel I was alarmed to find I was sharing the same room with her. Twin beds and huge ones at that. I thought of my ragged pyjamas, my inclination to snore as I looked indignantly at her exquisite nighty, until she put it on and then in turning, I saw she had a huge hole in the back of it. That cheered me up enormously. I felt more equal and I donned my rags with less embarrassment, slipped into bed, and I am ashamed to admit was fast asleep before Millicent had half finished her elaborate toilet for the night.... At about nine or ten (next morning) she phoned for breakfast, and we shared bacon and toast and coffee. It must be remembered that Millicent never started the day much before twelve. She was not allowed to, owing to her heart condition that so worried us, which made me look up apprehensively at her whenever I woke up, in the night or morning. After dressing she would sit up, wherever she was, hotel or tent, and "put on her face", her extraordinary subtle make up. Then she would proceed to swallow a handful of assorted pills of all colours." [101]

Dorothy Brett.
(Courtesy *Three Women* by William Goyen.)

Frank Waters also wrote about this time remodeling the house. "To work on her house Millicent employed several Indians, including a young man who had returned from war dissolute, alcoholic, angry, and violent. She became infatuated with him, paid all his successive debt, and took him with Brett to Jamaica. Upon their return, and in late afternoons after work, all these Indians sat in the house drinking and cutting slices from the huge roast beef always available. How pleasant it was for Tony to join them! Not until late at night did he return home, well fed and smelling of scotch. Mabel ate a solitary dinner and went to bed seething with anger and jealousy."

Other Taoseños who worked on Turtle Walk were Mark Romero, who was recommended by Lieutenant Commander Dicus, and Ralph Vigil. Taos master adobe plasterer Carmen Velarde recalls that some of the fireplaces in Turtle Walk were worked on by her grandmother and grandfather. "I was still young. They plastered fireplaces, fire walls. They used terra blanca and terra colita. I still know how to mix the earth adobe. The plaster had to be mixed a certain way with straw. We used to work with Kiker too, before her, plastering the outside of the house. Grandpa would mix the mud. I imagine Trinidad was there. He was a good friend. She (Millicent) was very kind to the Indians and Hispanics. She would bring me coloring books and crayons and books from wherever she traveled–to the Indian kids also. We didn't have those available in Taos then."[102]

The crests on the front gate and garage are from a Medici palace that Millicent's grandfather had imported to Southampton. They lay in the old slave dungeons at Claremont before Millicent brought them to Taos.

Library in Turtle Walk. (Courtesy Arturo Peralta-Ramos III.)

Crest from the Medici Palace at Turtle Walk. (Courtesy Arturo Peralta-Ramos III.)

The magnificent solid Italian marble bathtub, dating to 25 A.D., in the guest suite at Turtle Walk came from Florence, Italy, via Fairhaven and Southampton, to Claremont, where it sat in a garage until 1949. When it was shipped to Taos, Millicent decided she did not want to use it in the house, so it sat on the side of the hill for almost 50 years. Years later, when Jackie Peralta-Ramos lived in the house, she had it moved into the guest bathroom. A large hole in side of the wall had to be made to hoist it in. Guests love to bathe in it. One evening while Arturo and Jackie were hosting a dinner party, they heard a man screaming for help. All the guests rushed in to see the man writhing in agony as he'd let the plug out before he got out of the tub; and the strong draining whirlpool sucked his testicles into the drain. He could not move because every time he wiggled he got sucked in deeper. Roaring with laughter, everyone tried to think of what to do. Eventually Jackie suggested that he use a large salad spoon with lard as a lubricant. He worked the spoon in and was able to slip out of the tub.[103]

Books were Millicent's world. Her "annotated" library at Turtle Walk is a magnificent eclectic collection reflecting excellent taste in literature.

She read a book first thing every morning. When Millicent got cold, she would take a rug off the floor or wall and use it as a wrap. Another aspect of her creativity is that Millicent was a knitter. She also dyed materials for use in clothing and household fabrics.

"She loved camping too for she was so happy and entirely free. And we did not think to take her to a Navajo 'Sing,' to their strange healing ceremonies, for the powerful medicine men to try to cure her heart. They said, after she was so ill in the Fonda Hotel, with the

Roman marble bathtub in Turtle Walk (Courtesy Arturo Peralta-Ramos III.)

infection of the heart valves, that if we took her to them they would give a 'Sing' for her, but by then she was too fragile to travel so far."[104]

Millicent, Brett, Paul, Arturo, Dusty, Trinidad Archuleta, and Benny Suazo would go camping up in

Tony Lujan's cabin high in the mountain near the top of the road to Raton to camp. They cooked and ate freshly caught trout, bacon, hash browns, and baked beans for dinners. There were typical cowboy-type breakfasts with Paul, Arturo, or Trinidad doing the cooking. The men used sleeping bags outside and the women slept inside. Arturo bought an old military weapons carrier that was used to haul all the gear for camping.

According to Arturo II, "Mabel was always asked by MR to go on these trips, but Mabel would snap, 'I'm not going up to that dirty cabin.' Mother respected Mabel because she brought so many people together. Mabel was a meddler. We all adored Frieda. We loved Brett."[105]

Arturo relates, after one of the camping trips, "Only once we went to a Jicarilla Apache ceremony at their lake where I took her, Brett, Trinidad, Benny, Dixie and John Yaple in my WWII weapons carrier and Yaple's truck…two Indian teepee tents, sleeping bags and tons of food brought by MR in large wicker type English picnic baskets. This is where she tried Peyote with everyone and danced by large built Indian wood fires and sang with the Indians until late into the night, with nearly everyone spaced out.

Taos was now Millicent's major residence al-though she often traveled to her other homes in New York and Jamaica. Arturo tells of a time when Millicent, Paul, and himself traveled to Jamaica:

"Jamaica 1948: nearing the end of the winter season, when most people closed their homes, Mother would throw a large masquerade beach party on Louis Reynolds private walled-in, white, sandy beach near the airport at Montego Bay. On the one remaining old block

Kitchen in Turtle Walk. (Courtesy Arturo Peralta-Ramos III.)

Millicent's bedroom in Turtle Walk. (Courtesy Arturo Peralta-Ramos III.)

View of Taos Mountain from garden gate at Turtle Walk.
(Courtesy Arturo Peralta-Ramos III.)

Guest bedroom with the vigas painted by Brett and Trinidad.
(Courtesy Arturo Peralta-Ramos III.)

Millicent dying material in the Tony House. (Courtesy Millicent Rogers Museum.)

stone fisherman ruins that was left, the smell of vines of bougainvillea, the shrubs of various assortment, and of orchids saturated and permeated always the cool, ocean-breezed night air. On this occasion she decided to have a 'Cannibal Party.' She arranged to have the native artisans build an actual reproduction miniature African village.

Trinidad Archuleta, Millicent, and Charles Harding McCarthy at Apache Lake, 1949. (Courtesy Millicent Rogers Museum.)

This consisted of twelve small straw huts placed in an outer circle facing and encircling three large open straw, chieftain huts. Then in the center were placed three large iron cauldrons filled with bubbling water on large log cooking fires.

Since Mother had a rather creative and imaginative sense of humor, she arranged a few days before the big dinner to give Paul, myself, and twelve of our peers a barbeque dinner at the Wharf House, her enchanting home across Montego Bay. The conditions were that each of us was to be given a large coconut that we were to carve grotesque faces on. When we asked why, she innocently stated that she needed these heads for the party. Paul, not totally satisfied with her response, shot back, 'That's no answer–what for?'

For an instant she contemplated whether to reply, then with a big, smirking smile on her face she explained that at the party each of us would have fifteen minutes to chose one of twelve of the best costumed native servants there. The chosen twelve would then have fifteen minutes to secretly and independently choose the three best carved heads between them. The three winners would split a prize of $1,000 in a 40% / 30% / 20% plus 10% would go to the winning carver. That 10% to one of us made the creative carving very competitive, and jealously guarded, by each of us until all were completed! Secretly, and unbeknownst to any of us, the coconut heads were to be placed eerily floating grotesquely upwards in the bubbling water of the middle cooking cauldron prior to the arrival of the guests.

In the three main chieftain huts were placed long wooden bamboo tables to hold every type of wondrous food and exotic drink found on and around Jamaica Island. There were shell fish of every type, large and small, even cockle shells still clinging to the fresh green, salty seaweed. Wild boar, chicken, goats, lamb, and beef steaks were prepared in a dozen different ways as well as alligator meat from the numerous semi-un-explored swamp areas of the island. Laid out in lavish display were coconuts, mangoes, oranges, bananas, and grapefruit – all of the fruits of that luscious, producing paradise island. All types of permitted forms of birds and sweet tasting lizard and frogs were found encased in banana leaves. The entire walkways to and from the huts were covered by glimmering hand-made bamboo torches, reflecting the entire area in a mysterious shadowed flickering of light.

Dave Cordova. Brett's painting done in Jamaica. (Courtesy Arturo Peralta Ramos II.)

Staff members, waiters, cooks, and bartenders from numerous stores, private homes, small lodges, beach hotels, and even off-duty members of the local constabulary played the necessary roles of tribal cannibals to help serve the guests. Each of these individuals, delightedly, came in the appropriate cannibal costumes supplied by Mother. The dancers and musicians came in wild, appropriate costumes and played the wildest of savage African music. Even the on-duty constables arrived in tribal outfits with beautifully painted shields and feathered mounted spears. They were there to ascertain the proper invited guest list and, more importantly, to be 100% sure 'NO guest would leave in an unattainable walking movement.' Those that failed the mental or walking test, were ushered politely over to their awaiting chauffeured car or a stand-by friendly taxi cab.

When all was in order, the invitations went out by telegram as the phone system in Jamaica in those days was like waiting for an egg to hatch! Each telegram had to be responded to by a return telegram within 48 hours or one's name was removed. It was well known that one could not pass the entrance gate of the 'Reynolds Private Guarded Beach' otherwise.

MR's Telegram: You are honorably Invited to a BARBEQUED CANNIBAL DINNER 15th Moon Day of March – Moment of Greenwich Darkness Till Rise of Sun. Appropriate Dress Mandatory.

Best Reply: Delighted to come to eat. Who are we having for dinner? Signed: Noel Coward.

The Dinner; Everyone arrived in various imaginative costumes. Mother was in a complete Witch Doctor's regalia of a diverse assortment of wildly colored feather, beads, and an mélange of sea shells strung around her long neck. From her waist hung tiny shrunken skulls. Her face and hand were covered in bright gold and her finger nails were painted shiny black. Her blondish hair was mixed and entwined with sea weed. She truly looked evil and fit the part. Not one person, man or woman, failed to arrive not fitting the active part.

Departure: All safely including those found sleeping in huts or covered by mounds of sand.

Worst Exit: 'Bobby! Bobby! Someone's theft my steering wheel!' Politely the constable replied, 'No Sir. **You in back seat!**'[106]

Again Arturo II reminisces about Jamaica, "In 1950 MR took Brett, Trinidad Archuleta, and Benito Suazo to Jamaica. Millicent was invited to a party given by the British Governor General. She asked if she could bring her Indian friends and was told that it was a formal affair. MR had Trinidad and Benito fitted for tuxedos. When she went to pick them up, MR found they had cut the seat out of the pants and had their Indian blankets wrapped around their tux jackets so that their loin clothes and their bare butts showed! After dinner they performed ceremonial dances for the guests, but they left their blankets on.

"While in Jamaica, Brett painted. Jackie Peralta-Ramos has one of her paintings from that time. Also, when the Indian friends became drunk the Jamaican constabulary would call for MR, 'Come pick up your Indians.'"[107]

Revelers at the Cannibal party in Jamaica.
(Courtesy Arturo Peralta-Ramos II.)

In Taos, Millicent, like most mothers, never stopped being anxious for her children. In a letter she typed to Paul that mirrors the letter she received from her own father, the Colonel, she wrote:

Taos, New Mexico
August 5, 1952

Dearest Paulie:

I am very worried about you. I think you have set up your trust monies wrong–you have a large amount of cash at one point and nothing at another, and as you are not used to keeping accounts you are again, this month, short. As you will always be if you do it quarterly.

I am sending you $100.00 so that you can eat, not to squander, but don't imagine you are getting around me because I send it to you. I would like to help you straighten yourself out. My suggestion to you would be that you have your money come in to you each month, and that you allocate certain sums for laundry, for food, electricity, telephone, etc., whatever you need and the remaining to go into your piggy bank for you to spend in any way you choose.

My helping you out this month does not mean that I will pay your rent if you race; this I told you when we talked of it over the phone. I sent Dixie a word when she was in New York so that she would know what was going on and be able to talk to you about it which I understand she has done. What did you think I was saying, I wonder.

I would think you would understand that I have very large increases in debts since my illness and I frankly see no reason why you should expect me to do everything to help you, when you do nothing in exchange. Life isn't run that way–not for very long in any event. It would appear that I have great obligations to you and Arthur (Arturo II), but neither of you feel that you have any toward me.

You must have understood what I was saying after Dixie read the telegraph to you, even if, for some strange reason you entirely failed to interpret our conversation over the phone re: rent.

I told you that I would not advise you to go into business as an employee of Mr. K., as Mr. K. has an extremely bad reputation, which would very likely reflect on you. He wouldn't offer you a job for your big eyes! Furthermore, as you know nothing of antiques, I suppose he would want you to get my custom, or something of the sort. Never in my wildest dreams would I have told you that I would pay you for not working. It is utterly incredible that you thought up something like that to say to me on the phone. I repeat that I see no reason why I should put myself more in debt by paying your rent, if you have sufficient income to race cars and do all the things that pertain to racing. I know from experience with your father whose bills I paid in that regard, that it is an extremely expensive hobby and you have no capital for it.

I don't like your breaking your word to me. The beginning of September you will have to take care of your own rent. I can't understand how you could have possibly lied to me in this respect. I am heart-sick, discouraged and disgusted-a word given, whether over the phone or verbally, is as binding as one written on paper, maybe not legally, but certainly as a gentleman.

Affectionately,
M.R.

MAR:DLY
Encl/

P.S. I won't go into what I have paid Arthur and Dusty, although Dusty (Arturo II and his first wife Dusty) says that I treat Arthur as a step-child, but I can tell you what I have paid during the eight month of this year for you:

Taxes: Last ¼ 1951 Est. Fed. Tax	*$216.60*	
Bal. of 1951 Fed. Tax		*493.25*
First ¼ 1952 Est. Fed. Tax	*400.00*	
1951 New Mex. Inc. Tax	*53.60*	
		$1,165.45
Allowance: January thru May – 5 mos.	*2,750.00*	
Medical: January thru July 1952	*948.03*	
Rent: January through August	*325.00*	
Hotel Exp. In Santa Fe	*184.70*	
Telephone – January & Feb.		*19.81*
Cash		*100.00*
		$5,992.99

This does not include the $525.00 commission paid to you for the sale of "The Spanish Dancers", and is also aside from the trusts I made for you. In addition I will have to pay taxes on this amount paid to you since there is a limit as to what may be given an individual as a gift.

I gave you a good education, and I was glad to do it. I would like to have had you both go through college, so that you could stand on your own feet. That you both failed to take advantage of your op-portunities, so that now, you have no qualifications in getting jobs, does not mean that my duty is to support you both every time you run into trouble. I made trust large enough to keep you going (without great hardship) if you worked. I think my duty ends there, so when

you put on a high hat over the phone, I think less than nothing of it,
for you can see before you the extras that you have so far gotten this year.

M. A. R.

P.S.S
Adding the commission to the other expenses it barely covers the price
of your new racing car!!! And in this I will have to pay the government
a large tax as one can't give away more than $1,800.00 a year!"[108]

In 1954 Paul wrote:

"*M. R. was what I called her. I think I gave Mother this name*
because I didn't want to call her Mummy or Mother. I wanted her
more as an equal than a parent who could tell me what I could do or
couldn't do. She never did, however, dictate any demands: in racing
she merely refused to pay bills because she said I had $550 a month
and I could get along if I gave up racing. She would use humiliation
as an end at some point she wanted to put across. Watkins Glen
(race course) she told them I was under 21 and had the lawyer do it.
However, she did telegraph it was O.K. when I called up and let her
know I wanted to do it.

She did make me laugh. She would tell a story sometimes on
herself or her parents which were terribly amusing. This she did the
last four months before her death.

I must say I adored her. She was very beautiful (when young)
then after took great care always to do her face well–very stunning
in dress along with beautiful jewelry (sic) which was very impressive
to me. However, I was always embarrassed at school because other
parents never looked as beautiful. Her taste was superb in Fine Arts
and Antiques. She was always praised by Museum people on this.

She was very intellectual and modern in her thinking. Great
minds as Huxley, Spencer, Erin Rand (Ayn Rand) would always be
seen in her house or houses. She liked modern art and knew all or
most of the artists.

This side I liked in her as I also have some of these interests and would like to have the faculties to know and interest important and interesting people. I always have liked new and revolutionary ideas? (Paul's punctuation)

M. R. was one of the kindest persons I have ever known to animals, with the exception of cockroaches. In Va., she never allowed snakes to be killed. The most decrepit beasts would be seen.

I always liked her new interests. African art was one – or living in Taos where the Indians were. She never stayed in one spot.

As I think of it now, she moved because of a man as a rule. To a new place or departing from a place. This may not be true.

I often feared her. I don't know why. Discipline, I suppose. I must admit I adored her good taste in things. And ability to assemble them together without a clash.

When she had a boy-friend, one in particular, I was immensely jealous and at one time revealed he was with another woman when she thought him somewhere else. (I liked the guy). He was around 35 and fun to be with.

I hated most of all the Indian who lived in the house. I don't think they ever stayed together but I did anything to catch them together. But I never found it out. I hated most of all what people said about her behavior with this man. He was a drunk and I think she thought she could help him. People talked very badly of her because of this."[109]

Millicent helped many local people. She took Isabelle Concha under her wing, and from a cook, Isabelle became her personal nurse. Millicent sent Isabelle to Albuquerque for nurses' training, and she had to wear a nurse's uniform when she came back to work for Millicent. After that Isabelle was with her all the time. She would give Millicent a glass of water while Millicent took her pills one at a time. Isabelle told her children that she thought no matter how much money and fame Millicent had, she was often lonely or alone. Isabelle comforted Millicent when she got low or was bothered by "the ghost." Isabelle never said a harsh thing about Millicent, and she used to laugh about how she gave Millicent a fry bread lesson, although Millicent never did make it on her own. [110]

Dave Cordova. Portrait of Isabella Luhan by Julian Robles.
(Courtesy Julian Robles.)

Arturo states that while ghosts have been seen on three occasions in the guest bedroom, it was of an elderly Hispanic gentleman in a black suit and white shirt. Pueblo legend says that Turtle Walk was built over an old Spanish cemetery.

Another person she helped was Benito Suazo. She started Benito in the designing and making of jewelry. There were many rumors about Millicent's relationship with Benito, but none can be substantiated other than she cared for him almost like a son. Brett, in her essay, tells of the time Benito totaled Millicent's '47 Chrysler:

"One night tho, (after a party) the Indian boy (Benito) who drove Millicent's car had had a little too much drink and I insisted on taking her home. It was bitterly cold. This was a dance (All of Millicent's Indian dances were given in Brett's studio) she gave around Christmas time. The boy got into her car and drove off a bit too fast. We followed, and to be sure enough, a mile or so down the road, Millicent saw her car in a ditch. We got out to find him in the front seat unconscious, a large telephone pole right across the top of the car. The car was a pulp. At last a car came along and some men helped us get the boy out into my station wagon. With one of the men to help, I drove to the hospital. There he was taken to the X ray room. His ribs were broken, so I drove Millicent home while her chauffer got the police and did all the necessary things with them. It was six in the morning when we got home.

For weeks after that, every afternoon, about four, and many evenings after supper, I would drive Millicent to the hospital where she would care for the boy and look after him. She had always wanted to be a doctor, but her health never permitted her to take up such an arduous profession. She was patient, gentle, and seemingly tireless. I would go to sleep in a chair in the hall of the hospital until she was ready to go home. He was a difficult, strange boy coming out of the war, as so many did, bruised and hurt and morose. Many people attempted to rehabilitate this boy. None had succeeded, not even Millicent with all her kindness."[111]

At other times Millicent gave parties in her home and patio. During one of the early fancy parties she gave, two busloads of Pueblo Indians and artists arrived.

In a 1951 letter that Frieda Lawrence wrote to Witter Brynner, she said, "Millicent's party was very beautiful with the Indians dancing under that enormous sky round a fire, and lightening, and a few drips of rain, and an enormous moon. …I like her so much."[112]

In 1950 Millicent gave a Thanksgiving dinner. Lois Rudnick states in her book about Mabel, *Mabel Dodge Luhan, New Woman, New Worlds*, "…Mabel was invited…one of the art patronesses and hostesses of Taos. This Thanksgiving she had managed to capture one of Hollywood's leading actresses–Moira Shearer, who had just completed *Red Shoes* and was on her way out to Hollywood to make *Hans Christian Anderson* with Danny Kaye. Rogers also invited several Indians, and other local notables, besides Brynner and Mabel to dinner. By the time Brynner arrived, the 'Indians were pretty well smashed and the scene was something out of Hogarth's Rake's Progress.' Brynner thought that Mabel had refused to come to the party, but Millicent informed him that she was 'holding court alone in the ante-room.' He apparently decided that their antagonism had gone on long enough and went out to greet her. They had a long talk and 'made up.' He then convinced Mabel to come in and join the party. According to the friend of Brynner's who recounted this story, Mabel had clearly, by the end of the evening, lost her title to 'Queen of the Mountain.'"[113]

Miranda Levy related about the Thanksgiving party: "The library had just been completed. It was absolutely gorgeous. There was a Thanksgiving meal table from one end of it to the other. The scene was so surreal with the Indians holding up greasy drumsticks."[114]

Benito and Trinidad were left money in Millicent's will. Benito was found frozen to death along the road between Taos and the Pueblo within a year of Millicent's death.

Arturo II and Paul made sure Brett was well taken care of after Millicent's death. In June 1953 they paid for her to attend the coronation of Queen Elizabeth II. In photos from the time Brett can be seen sitting in the enclosure for peers in Westminster Abby. One time Jackie went to visit Brett and found her with mouse bites on her arms and a rattlesnake curled under her bed. Her bookcases were covered with wire to keep the mice from eating the books. Jackie and Arturo II took Brett home for ten days while they had her house completely cleaned and disinfected.

Millicent arranged for an exhibition of Brett's paintings at the American British Art Gallery in New York and was her constant art patron for the rest of her life.

The correspondence between Brett and Millicent was extensive, showing the trust between the friends. A great number of the letters from Brett to Millicent have been lost. Excerpts from Millicent's letters to Brett:

• *Can't write. Hand has gone bad. Hear Mabel selling things from the big house. Too sad! Steal for me the picture of Tony going up the ladder when he was young. Have been very sick but better now. To hell with spells.*

• *As for thinking of the gods as Lawrence (D.H.) he seems a little thin and skimpy for a ... deity.*

• *Regarding companions for travel I prefer the Indians. I like their moods and silence and singing.*

• *The white men have lost the core and they have filled it up with the dollar.*

• *(regarding Benito) I like him, know him. What Taos thinks is no concern to me. His cot in my room. I like Indians, I like the feeling of safety they engender. You write about Benito to my Paulie. Benny took care of me in ways that paid help would never have done. The pleasures, like having someone light the fire or walk across the floor with a light step. It's high time you stopped all this nonsense about Benny. You keep stirring up my children and their friends. The household and the spirit of the house has been upset all summer.*

• *Tony (Lujan) saying "White people talk too much, feel too little, flies buzzing."*

• *What's this about a spirit in the Tony House? What kind of spirit? Dixie (Yaple) was always going on about it! Very lonely or sad or something. I hate to miss anything. I don't see any reason why a bad spirit should sit in any house of Tony's.*

• *Don't worry-I don't care what they write about me. I've never met the woman they write about.*

• *How is the dear Trinidad...I must say I didn't like the shade of green we've put on that ceiling - it's too much like arsenic. But it can be washed down I dare say.*

• *I hear that Xmas Eve was heaven at the Pueblo. How I shall miss the Deer Dance. The only thing is that next year it will come again.*

• *You are quite right the hammerings (hammering her jewelry) is frightfully hard and hurts my shoulder - it would be fine to get helpers eventually. Only what makes you think Ralph Meyers' two Indians would make silversmiths?*

• *The thing about New York is the amount everyone talks. I get restless with all those voices going at once.*

• *We dash through life afraid of missing something-while the things we look for stand quietly.*

• *Don't get upset - I wired Dixie at the same time as I did you ...So I can't understand what it's all about. It's as if I was posted like a game preserve - No Poaching on this property - Trespasser will be prosecuted by the law.*

• *How you could imagine that I would tolerate a man like that Romanian... He is not male enough to please me. He goes about speaking of how many women he has spent his time with... I like men who do not question themselves.*

• *The idea of leaving Taos doesn't please me but perhaps I can't think always of myself and really until I came to Taos I was more or less always on the move. My father was the same way and mother too – so that we went to Europe, to China to Africa and the South Americas and up & down all kinds of places. It must have been horrid when you went back home finding everything different, that's in a way why I don't want to go back to the place I've lived in and been happy.*

• *You ask what a male man is - well it's hard to say isn't it. Everyone has different opinions. I should say all the Indians are supremely male-men. To me it's a man who doesn't need to say how many conquests he's made, someone who is so unconsciously male... and I think that is when a man has sufficient of the female in him as to be wise and gentle and capable.*

• *Tonight I'm sure someone was singing for me - it was ...8:30 your time. Such sudden strength came through as sometimes does come from the mountain when they sing. You Know. There is nothing else like it, one can't mistake...*

• *Life is so damn boring if one is too efficient.*

• *I wonder if Trinidad would make a good luck for my friend Jimmy Daniels who is a... night club owner and singer - and an old friend of 22 years - an angel of goodness and kindness and light.*

• *Claremont and the Port get upset with ghosts when certain winds blow.*

• *I always wish white men had long hair. Long black hair is wonderful. It always gets me in the middle of the tummy in a funny way. It has something so strong about it, so male and powerful. It has some of the mountain power about it.*

• *The children want to go to Europe this summer, maybe in August I hope to take them. It might teach them a lot America can't.* [115]

"Earl Stroh, one of the most respected artists in Taos, briefly met Millicent in New York when he was working for the British-American Art Center. A perfectionist, he was impressed to find the same quality in her when they were reacquainted in Taos. 'There was one door that led into what she called her Turtle Room,' Stroh says. 'I don't know how many times she had that door moved, a few inches one way, a foot another. She had the door, frame and everything torn down and replaced until she found the proper place and it pleased her eye. She was always right.

"'When she had her art collection trucked from her home in Virginia, I was delighted to find a superb Derain and a Rouault, also a Whistler and Tchelitchew. The range of her collection was interesting. I remember a Benin bronze in the library and the dining room held a surprise–a Renoir still life in a vase, one of the most sumptuous Renoirs I've ever seen. It was if the painter had invited Van Gogh and Rubens to participate. I don't know how Millicent expected her guests to concentrate on conversation or dinner while looking at the painting. You couldn't take your eyes from it.

"Stroh, at the time, was a young struggling artist living in a hovel with one naked light bulb and a privy outside. Millicent dropped in and bought seven of his works. True or not, she had a reputation of not paying her bills promptly, but in this case her driver arrived with a check the next morning." Stroh was her consultant on American Western Art.[116]

In a letter to Brett, Millicent exclaimed about her own exhibition of jewelry in New York: "Well–the exhibition is a great success. The opening was packed and with such unexpected people, like Georgia O'Keefe. I can't remember if I told you the ballet came and all the museum heads … and Noguchi and hundreds of people from the design school (Parsons School of Design). I can't see entirely why, but it's just gone over big and not from any social, society, chic, *Vogue Magazine*, newspaper point of view, from a professional viewpoint. Amazing. I've even been given a few orders."[117]

"The first thing one noticed in Millicent's Taos home was that her bedroom was oversized and appeared to be more of a sitting room. In truth, it was her salon, with a big window capturing the expanse of a nearby mountain (Taos Mountain). 'The family would sit around, read magazines and talk,' Paul remembers, 'It was never considered a sickroom. She'd been ill almost all of her life, and both she and the rest of us knew it and took it for granted. At one point she suffered a stroke on her left side

Judith Bronner. Taos Pueblo, North Village. (Courtesy Cliffshooter Photography.)

and she made herself work on her jewelry, dealing with large hunks of metal, and using the wax technique which entailed her pushing the metal into the wax with all her strength. Eventually, there were little or no side effects from the stroke. She was a woman who expected as much or more of herself as she did of others.

"When she moved back to America during World War II, Millicent began a close collaboration with American fashion designer Charles James, who made hundreds of ball gowns, dresses, blouses and other garments for Millicent. In 1948, after moving to Taos, she donated her collection of James gowns and fashions to the Brooklyn Museum. She also made designs, worked with, and was friends with Elsa Schiaparelli, Coco Chanel, Adrian, Edith Head, Mainbocher, Verdura, Cartier, Valentina, and John Schulumberger.

"The great designer Charles James and mother both had a wonderful sense of humor and he always lifted her spirits. Once he visited when she was feeling low and he had a bad case of hiccups. He told her she looked terrible and that her hair was a rat's nest and said she must be depressed. She agreed that she was. Then he got on the phone, hiccups and all, called Jennifer Jones in California, and arranged for her hairdresser to come out to Taos. I picked up the lady at the Albuquerque airport, drove her back and she did Mother's hair. It really perked her up. The entire episode was very funny. Here was this dying woman and a hiccupping man, and what did they do but send for a hairdresser."[118]

63 - Iratton symbol -
69 - Surprise.
70 - 2 Bracelets Navaho design -
71 - The Three Brothers (Belt) x
72 - the crocodile and the birds (necklace)
73 - Death Song of the Black Hills (necklace)
74 - Sun and Rays - (necklace.
75 - Nugget cuff links -
96 - Weaving Chains - (Bracelet.)
77 - Bead Lightning - (Buckle) x
    "   "   -   (Pin)
78 - 6 (figures - pins) the Happy ones - x
79 - the Mask of the Red Death x
                    (Wax)
x means not yet in -

I sent you both no used
Here section to amuse you
incase the notice is late.

JEWELRY Do you
      BY   — like the
                names

MILLICENT ROGERS

May two through May twenty-eight
1949

DURLACHER BROS
11 EAST 57th STREET

PINS AND CLIPS

1944	51	WINGED SERPENTS
"	52	GOLD ORCHID
"	53	GOLD FLAMING HEART
"	54	WEREWOLF
1945	55	PLANT AND ROOT
"	56	OBIA
1946	57	THE INDIAN
1945	58	THE LAUGHING TREE FACE
"	59	WATER FACE
"	60	RAM'S HEAD
"	61	FOUNTAIN FACE
"	62	ROCK FACE
"	63	THE FAUN
"	64	THE SATYR
		Nos. 52 to 64 lent by Peter Salm, Esq.

MISCELLANEOUS

1946	65ᵇ	ANDROMEDA (figure) Lent by Mrs. D. H. Lawrence
1946	66	MEDUSA (paper weight)
1947	67	REMEMBERED FACE (box)

ROOTS BY MRS. JAN GOODWIN
WOVEN BANDS BY OLI & JOAN SIHVONEN

BRACELETS

1949	1	RAIN ON ICE
1945	2	THE EARTH MOTHER'S Bracelet
1948	3	MAGIC CORN
1946	4	SPEAK NO EVIL
1943	5	WINTER MAGIC
1946	6	WOOD WITH HOAR FROST Lent by Peter Salm, Esq.
1946	7	DISC BRACELETS
	8	WOOD CHAIN

BUTTONS AND BUCKLES

1946	9	THREE YELLOW BUTTONS Lent by Mrs. John C. Wilson
1946	10	LILY PAD Lent by Mrs. Henry Field
1944	11	EMBRYO MERMAID
1947	12	ARROW HEAD
1947	13	LION FACE
1945	14	FROZEN LEAF
1947	15	MUSHROOM STUDS
1946	16	LOW TIDE
1946	17	THE WEDDING BELT
1949	18	ARROW PATH BELT
1946	19	ROCK PILE (earrings) Lent by Miss Margaret Mallory

NECKLACES AND PENDANTS

1949	20	APACHE MOON FIGURES
"	21	SUNSET STRAWS
"	22	DARK MOTLEY
1948	23	IDOL TRAPPED
"	24	LOST LIZARD
1949	25	COLD SEA AND EARTH
1948	26	SUN - MAN - CORN
1947	27	WINTER SILVER
"	28	WINTER MAGIC
1946	29	GOLD LANDSCAPE
1947	30	CORN FROG IN MOONLIGHT
"	31	RED — WILLOW — SUN
1946	32	FIGURES OF GROWTH
	33	GOLDEN CIRCLES Lent by Peter Salm, Esq.
1947	34	MOON DISCS Lent by Mrs. James Johnson
1949	35	OUT OF AFRICA

RINGS

1949	36	"TRUE LOVE?"
1948	37	MUSHROOM RING Lent by Mrs. Benjamin Rogers
1948	38	HIGH HAT
1946	39	HONEY SQUARE
1945	40	FAINT FACE
1945	41	GOLDEN FACE Lent by Miss Ethel Shaw
"	42	EARTH Lent by Joseph Fried, Esq
"	43	ROCK RING Lent by Mrs. John C. Wilson
"	44	THE BENT ROCK
"	45	HONEY GOLD Lent by Mrs. Mathilde C. Seif
1946	46	MAGIC STALK Lent by Mrs. James Johnson
1947	47	GOLDEN POOL Lent by Comtesse Elizabeth de Breteuro
1940	48	LEAVES OF SUMMER Lent by Miss Margaret Mallory
"	49	DRAGON Lent by Mrs. Van Day Truex, Esq.
"	50	YELLOW DOME RING Lent by Miss D. D. Dixon

Brett's copy of the invitation to Millicent's show at Durlacher Bros. Gallery,
New York, 1949. (Courtesy The Harry Ransom Center, University of Texas, Austin.)

Bruce Gomez. Taos Pueblo with snow. (Courtesy Bruce Gomez.)

FINAL RESTING PLACE

Millicent Rogers attended every major Indian dance and San Geronimo feast on the Taos Pueblo, including the Christmas Eve bonfires and Christmas Day Deer Dance, the week before she died. She died on January 1, 1953, at 6:30 a.m., a month short of her 51st birthday, in Albuquerque, after surgery for an aneurysm.

"She didn't die because of her heart," Dorothy Brett wrote. "She fell down and hit her head against the bathtub over Christmas. She had a black eye but didn't think anything of it. Then her brain started hemorrhaging and she was operated on and lasted one day. ... she died of a massive stroke. It would take something like that to do in M-R. She didn't believe in limitations and time was her only enemy."[119]

The autopsy showed her heart was four times the normal size. She was buried in the Sierra Vista cemetery in Taos wrapped in a rare Navajo blanket and wearing two neo-primitive rings. "Pallbearers were Ralph Vigil, John Yaple, James Wilcox, John Shorty, Tony Reyna, and Saki Karavas. Honorary pallbearers were her physician Dr. Erich Hausner Santa Fe and Jerome W. Sinsheimer, New York, attorney."[120]

"After the funeral Peter Salm asked Miranda Levy to ride with him to the cemetery, and he asked her what his mother owed her at the Thunderbird. He insisted on taking care of the bill," states Arturo II.[121]

Trinidad's wife Rufina's father built a memorial for Millicent on Taos Mountain. To this day no one knows where to find it.

In a letter to Paul, Brett wrote on July 8, 1953, "Think what M. R. did, her courage, her persistence in her own beliefs, she built up her life, and whether we agree with her building or not is immaterial, with only a thread of health, she went her way. Now you do the same, because that is what you owe yourself."

When Millicent died, she had disinherited Arturo II from her personal assets because of a private dispute and left her wealth to Paul. Paul objected, saying this was unfair and demanded that the estate be divided equally. Then it was discovered that her personal estate was bankrupt, and she had left a debt of between $2 and 3 million, which Paul didn't know when he made his declaration. Arturo and Paul paid off the debts, and split the personal assets equally, including Millicent's collections.

Arturo's Account of the Disinheritance:

The paragraph about my disinheritance is partially correct. It may appear to the reader that MR was extraordinarily cold-blooded and ornery towards me. She was only belligerent to the Nazis!

When Art asked me about this disinheritance, I hesitated for quite a while and then told him the story. When I finished he roared with laughter, and asked if I would write the story down and give my permission to put in this book. I agreed, but still will not reveal the actual fact that led to the disinheritance in the first place.

It commenced in 1942 or '43 and took place on in an afternoon at her house on 68th Street in New York. I had just gotten home a few days earlier from school for Easter. Neither Peter nor Paul had yet arrived from their school. I was getting hell over a situation that happened at my school as she had received a letter from the Head master regarding the supposed serious occurrence.

The situation became quite heated between the two of us. Finally in anger I threw back at her a serious occurrence that involved her. She went through the roof and demanded an immediate apology, which I instantly refused to do! The situation became more heated and finally she stated, "If you do not immediately apologize, I will disinherit you in my will!"

I retorted, "Go ahead. I won't apologize. Period!" I got up and left the room, packed my bag, and went over to stay with my grandmother at her apartment.

Occasionally over the years Mother would half jokingly remind me in a less serious argument of the apology I still owed her. I would laughingly remind her, "No apology for the money." And so it remained until the early morning of 26 December 1952 when Mother's secretary Dixie Yaple notified me that Millicent had been knocked out in a bad fall, somehow hitting her head against the small low, old Mexican Colonial wooden doorway that she loved and that led into her bedroom.

According to the local doctor it appeared that she had possibly received a serious concussion as well as the cut on her forehead. He called for an ambulance to take her to Santa Fe for x-rays and to be examined by her heart doctor at the hospital there.

The following morning her doctor suggested that, though she was now fully conscious, her family should be called to come immediately as her condition appeared to be very serious. Peter, Paul, myself and then wife Dusty, 'Mummida' her mother, her brother's widow Diana Rogers, her two closest cousins, Ambassador Robert Coe and his brother Henry, and her long-time friend and lawyer from World War II days – Jerome Sinsheimer- and Jimmy Wilcox, the nephew of Prince Felix Youssoupoff. We all found ways to get there at once from all parts of the U. S.

On the morning of 28th December, we all gathered at the hospital where a private sitting room, close to Mother's room, had been set up for us. At one point a nurse appeared and said the Mother wished to speak to Jerry Sinsheimer. Mummida became slightly disturbed as she felt she was the matriarch of the family and MR's mother and should be the first to see her, and certainly not her lawyer! Bobby Coe, being the next eldest, rose and went over to calm her down with great savior-faire.

In less than 15 minutes, Jerry poked his head around the door and looking straight at me stated, "Your mother wants to see and speak with you urgently now!"

Like a bolt of lightening Mummida was up out of her chair and angrily faced Jerry, "I am her mother and demand to see her now!"

With a polite composure he firmly informed Mummida that "Mrs. Rogers" needed to talk to me first. I followed him and shut the door behind us. If lightening struck the first time, an immediate burst of thunder came through the closed door from Mummida.

We got to Mother's room door and Jerry stopped and reached for a large envelope under his arm that contained two extremely long documents. One in each hand, he informed me that each was a final signed 'will' of Mother's estate. "One is you and Paul as the recipients of the estate, and the other is Paul as sole recipient with you legally disowned. Believe me Arturo I did all in my power as both long-time friend and legal advisor to do no such thing as to disinherit you. She only stated, emotionless, 'I will do nothing about this, with neither absolute love nor any malevolence. Only brother can make that definitive decision."

I remember very clearly how Jerry looked at me with a very sad expression and said, "For God's sake Arturo you have a wife and young son and a full life ahead of you. Don't be imprudent, she's dying so suppress your pride and fake your reply over whatever this is all about. Now we must go in as I must be the witness to your decision."

I was sadly shocked to see how frail and delicate she looked as she gently and slowly turned her head to see Jerry and myself. Her head was bandaged, covering the wound. A soft gentle smile appeared on her face, she spoke in a low, perceptive whisper as she made a slight movement with her right hand patting the bedside. She told me to sit on the bed next to her.

"Well, I guess I did it this time, but at least I got to see my last Deer Dance before I go. I always loved that Taos Indian Christmas dance, especially where there's snow on the ground and all the Indian men and women are in their most colorful women winter blankets. Well, I guess Jerry told you there are two wills for you to decide on finally."

I distinctly remember clearly the naughty smile that crossed her face. "MR nothing has changed. My answer is still 'N' 'O'. Therefore by disinheriting me you still won't win."

"Oh yes, I do because I told Jerry I knew which way you'd go. But what I would like to know now is why when you could have lied and gotten half my money."

We both looked at Jerry who was shaking his head in disbelief saying, "I don't believe the two of you. You're both insane."

She reached up her out-stretched hand, grasped mine, and asked, "But tell me why when all you had to do was fake and lie."

"MR I will tell you why, and there are quite a few reasons why I couldn't or wouldn't. You have always been a gambler, loving books of every form, studying art, history, and every type of religion and my reason is based on these presumptions. Though you are not religious and never have been, you had Peter, Paul, and myself

baptized as Catholics at birth. A little over a year ago you suddenly became Catholic based only on the possible gamble that millions of Catholics believe that only they go to Heaven or Hell while others don't get there and have to go to Purgatory first. So you had nothing to lose if it was not a fact. But if it is a fact, you certainly, discreetly so in your life, did enough to get there. So if Heaven is a fact and you are there, and I'd apologized, then you'd look down on me knowing, self-satisfied, I had falsely apologized simply for the money and not the true facts. In some way then you'd be able to communicate back down to me 'Fuck you. I got you in the end just for the money and not the true facts from our dispute years ago.' Hence, I'm gambling that you just might be right."

Jerry, again, shook his head and said, "You're both insane. I'd better get your mother in here now or she'll create holy hell in this hospital.

With that I kissed Mother good bye. The following mid-morning, she was moved down to the hospital in Albuquerque and was operated on for a massive brain aneurysm and died early the next morning on 1 January, 1953.[122]

Dixie Yaple suggested that Paul create a Museum to house his mother's exceptional collection of over 600 pieces of Native American and Pueblo jewelry, Pueblo pottery, textiles, basketry, Hispanic arts and crafts, and much more. Paul donated his collection of Millicent's art to the Museum. Arturo added a substantial portion of his collection. MBR and Peter Salm and other members of the family gave money every year to the Museum.

At first Brett offered her home for the museum, but it was much too small. A further description in *Taos Artists and Their Patrons* says, "Several years afterward, Brett as a generous tribute to her patron and friend, offered her home and studio to the Millicent Rogers Foundation. Although the gift never was realized, Paul Peralta-Ramos wrote, 'I think it is one of the most generous offers I have heard of in years…as fine a memorial to my mother as could be conceived.'"[123]

The first, temporary museum, according to the archives in the Millicent Rogers Museum, opened in temporary quarters on Ledoux Street in 1956. In the late 1960's, the Museum moved into its present home, a house built by Claude J. K. and Elizabeth Anderson and later donated to the Museum. The building was renovated and expanded in the mid-1980's by renowned architect Nathaniel A. Owings. The Peralta-Ramos family is still closely involved with the museum.

Peralta-Ramos family at the Millicent Rogers Museum. From left Ludi Salm (Peter's son), Shelly (friend of Phillip), Phillip Peralta-Ramos (Paul's son), Jackie Peralta-Ramos (Arturo's wife), Arturo Peralta-Ramos, Christina Peralta-Ramos Luera (Paul's daughter), Thomas Michael Luera (Christine's husband), and Antonia Salm (Peter's eldest daughter.) (Courtesy Arturo Peralta-Ramos II.)

Millicent had her friends carve their names in a step. It is now part of Gallery 12 in the Museum. The Millicent Rogers Museum Library is dedicated to John Joseph, Paul's tutor and life-long friend of the Rogers and Peralta-Ramos family. Even today, almost six decades after her death, she is credited with introducing what has become the Southwest look or the Santa Fe style.

When Paul Peralta-Ramos died in 2003, he was buried next to his mother, looking onto Taos Mountain. Paul had requested that he be buried in Fabergé boxes, and Arturo teased him by saying "We won't be able to tell which end of you is in which box! Besides it will be too expensive!"

Millicent wrote to Paul a few weeks before her death:

Darling Paulie,

Did I ever tell you about the feeling I had a little while ago? Suddenly passing Taos Mountain I felt that I was part of the Earth, so that I felt the Sun on my Surface and the rain. I felt the Stars and the growth of the Moon, under me, rivers ran. And against me were the tides. The waters of rain sank into me. And I thought if I stretched out my hands they would be Earth and green would grow from me. And I knew that there was no reason to be lonely that one was everything, and Death was as easy as the rising sun and as calm and natural– that to be enfolded in Earth was not an end but part of oneself, part of every day and night that we lived, so that Being part of the Earth one was never alone. And all fear went out of me–with a great, good stillness and strength.

If anything should happen to me now, ever, just remember all this. I want to be buried in Taos with the wide sky–Life has been marvelous, all the experiences good and bad I have enjoyed, even pain and illness because out of it so many things were discovered. One has so little time to be still, to lie still and look at the Earth and the changing colours and the Forest–and the voices of people and clouds and light on water, smells and sound and music and the taste of wood smoke in the air.

Life is absolutely beautiful if one will disassociate oneself from noise and talk and live it according to one's inner light. Don't fool yourself more than you can help. Do what you want–do what you want knowingly. Anger is a curtain that people pull down over life so that they only see through it dimly–missing all the savor, the instincts– the delight–they feel safe only when they can down someone. And if one does that they end by being to many, more than one person, and life is dimmed–blotted and blurred!–I've had a most lovely life to myself–I've enjoyed it as thoroughly as it could be enjoyed. And when my time comes, no one is to feel that I have lost anything of it–or be too sorry–I've been in all of you–and will go on Being. So remember it peacefully–take all the good things that your life put there in your eyes–and they, your family, children, will see through your eyes. My love to all of you.[124]

R.C. Israel. Mary Iron Eyes Painting, "Taos Rising." (Courtesy R.C. Israel.)

APPENDIX A

Handwritten letter by Millicent to Brett as an example of Millicent's handwriting.

Dearest Brett;

Dozens of letters of yours to
Answer. But till now its been a mad rush and
Answering questions - a sort of Gestapo asking &
Answering - Beginning sometimes before Breakfast,
to say that it has put me in a mad, agonized
fury is to put it mildly. I Hate to be pressed.
I hate to be expected to answer the unanswer-
able. to be expected to solve to unsolvable -

Well — the Exhibition is a great success —
the opening was packed - And with such over packed
people like Georgia O'Keefe. I can't remember
if I told you. The Ballet came, and all the
Museum Heads, And physco analists and Noguchi.
And Hundreds of people from design schools. I
Can't see entirely why, But its just gone over big
and hot from every Social, Society, chic Vogue
magazine, Newspaper point of view from a
professional Viewpoint - Amazing. I've even
Been given a few adees. (all from professional people !!! and that delights me.)

I've Had several adees for Whole Sale, and I think
in a few I'll give in. Luckily very few peoples' have
chosen the thing I personally like. and following
your precedent Ive put on these, Enormous prices
to scare them off. Even Ive Been asked to do a
Movie !!!! (not using my name) is not that too odd!
And an article on Symbolism - quite serious!

2

all of it. and again not because of name. over-
night I've become a professional which is so queer.
(But Satisfying.) So that I feel I have a much
more real foot Hold. only it's Confusing. As I
Haven't adjusted as yet which also upsets me.
I have to think Hard of the mountains and
all this Strong emanations - But being confused
in all this makes it more and more necessary to be
Quiet - which with moving Houses & so forth is Hard
as Bitter. and Leaves me Befuddled!

I will get all your guns & poles, logs and
Jackets and so forth & so on billed to morrow &
week - then I think I will go to Claremont for a
few days and sleep in the Hot, green, dampness of
Anguilla - then I shall come Home. truly I'm
very tired. But that is natural. also Surprised —
that so many people are interested in all this —

You are quite right the Hammering is frightfully
Hard. and Hurts my Shoulder - it would be fine to
get a Helper eventually. only what makes you
think Ralph Meyers two Indians would make
Silversmiths? they well might, I don't Know. we will
See - If Aliseo would come to let them Sooner
it would be fine. People are so indefinite -
He probably will Have gone Some where else —
although who Knows. Do ask Him. He seems
a good man. And I'm sure He would be Helpful

3

Why do you say - If I get angry with you to
say so.' - Why should I get angry with you? Of
course your Nerves is out why, if it that happ
But I can't some How see why. I don't think
Either of us are fighty - types. I'd along much
rather not fight with any Body. It makes
Me uncomfatable and sick. I'd much rather
like people. All people. only they so often go a
over nothing. Expecting too much more than any
me can give of manners and generousity. And so
Faith. Coupled with Hardness and taphness to.
Boot. Which means one Has to Concentrate o
them. More than is Healthy a interesting -
    As for money - it's this way. that I was
Brought up to think it common to Haggle over
a penny: and also to think most people Honest
As for Groceries. there are so many people w
are more interested in them than I am. I like
Very good food - n I don't Care - It doesn't matter
Me. I'd rather if necessary Have a glass of Milk
an egg and some Bread & Butter. and then for-
got it. I'm not a Buisness woman. And would
Be worse even if I Had not a penny - and do
you believe me. I'm not at all financialy n
I'm cracked up to Be. When I first got money
at My fathers death. I didn't like so much
of it - (which even than was it a 20th of what
is said -) it made me uncomfortable God

4

made trust for various people and did certain
things with it. her I have what the Bank gives
me. And it's Botten - I know, for when I think
what would I feel if I had it back. I - Have
the same kind of unhappy feeling inside - Some
Day I'll give all this up - and come into me
own what ever it is: I feel the teacher
has forgotten me lately. And that too con-
fuses me. But it maybe meant to Be.

I went into Connecticut last week and
found an Darl'am and we had a long talk.
And it was good inside again. I will tell y
later. He knew about my Great- great, great
Grand father so I felt at Home. there is trust
with them too - I wish they could all get together
then they would Be Heard. only they are so poor —
and Julian It's strange isn't it. with many our knew So
much of me Sick of Life. And when one is very po.
a whole other side - and I suppose it is difficult
know Both sides - at once - Certainly the poor who
have Become Rich have forgotten! maybe it is
only among the fundamental things - that me
has the whole Hardest Meeting - and that if one H
this, one has the most of all. I find, more and more
that I know very little indeed. well I'll go to
Bed now and I'll see you soon.

I'm glad Tony & Trised all have gone off dancing
I wish I could see and hear them - much trust you
and trust Bobs too h —

APPENDIX B

Homes Owned or Rented in Millicent's Life Time
Compiled by Arturo Peralta-Ramos
Many homes were owned outright or rented or lived or were lived in by both her mother and herself.

In the United States:

*	Fairhaven, MA	*
mar	New York City	1923
jnt	Southampton, NY	1912-30
jnt	Tuxedo Park, NY	1923-45
jnt	Palm Beach, FL	1923-45
rnt	Gloucester, MA	1943-44
jnt	Washington, D.C.	1942-45
mar	Southampton, NY	1943-52
mar	New York City	1940-50
mar	Claremont Manor, VA	1940
rnt	Beverly Hills, CA	1945-47
mar	Turtle Walk, Taos, NM	1948-53

In Europe:

rnt	Cannes, France	1933
mar	Gstaad, Switzerland	1933
mar	St. Anton, Austria	1935-39
jnt	Paris, France	1935-53
jnt	Rome, Italy	1934-38
jnt	Venice, Italy	1933-36
rnt	Brioni, Italy	1937
mar	Montego Bay, Jamaica	1945-53

Note 1 = ownership = mar ; Rented = rnt ; joint = jnt
Note 2 = Years are approximate

END NOTES

Chapter 1 – Early History

[1] Millicent's father, Colonel Henry Huddleston Rogers, who reverted to the old spelling of Huddleston with two "dds"

[2] Personal communication, Arturo Peralta-Ramos

[3] Ibid.

[4] Leary, Lewis, *Mark Twain's Correspondence with Henry Huttleston Rogers, 1893-1909*, University of California Press, Berkeley, 1969, pg. 600.

[5] Tisdale, Shelby J, *Fine Indian Jewelry of the Southwest: The Millicent Rogers Museum Collection*, Museum of New Mexico Press, 2006

[6] In naming her canary Yellow Peril Millicent shows an awareness of current affairs, and a sense of humor. Yellow Peril refers to the flood of Chinese immigrants who came to work on the railroads, and citizens saw them as a threat both culturally and economically. The term was later applied to the Japanese during World War II.

[7] The first time Millicent writes about the Germans, she spells Bosh incorrectly. Later in her diaries she spells Boche correctly. Boche is a pejorative word that the French used for the Germans, being a contraction of Kaboche, meaning "cabbage head."

[8] She inherited a $200,000 trust fund on the death of her grandfather, H.H. Rogers, of Standard Oil fame.

[9] Tapert, Annette and Edkins, Diana, *The Power of Style: The Women Who Defined the Art of Living Well*, Crown Press, 1994: 61

[10] Ibid.: 57

[11] *Fort Worth Star-Telegram*, 1920

[12] *Ogden Standard Examiner*, July 1921

Chapter 2 – The Rogers Family

[13] MacTaggart, Ross, *The Golden Century: Classic Motor Yachts, 1830-1930*, W.W. Norton & Co., NY, 2001:48

[14] Leary, Louis, ed. *Mark Twain's Letters to Mary*, Columbia University Press, 1961: 42

[15] *New York Evening Post*, May 29, 1907, refers to the Booker T Washington Papers: 124

[16] Personal communication, Arturo Peralta-Ramos II

[17] Adam Lewis, *Van Day Truex, The Man Who Defined Twentieth-Century Taste and Style,* Viking Studio, 2001:48-49.

[18] Ibid.: 111

[19] Fonda, Jane, *My Life So Far*, Random House, 2005: 26

[20] Ibid.: 28

Chapter 3 – Marriages and Sons

[21] Davis, Paul K. *100 Decisive Battles: From Ancient Times to the Present*, Oxford University Press, 2001:137.

[22] *Time Magazine*, March 13, 1939. When Count Ludwig Constantin Salm of Austria married Standard Oil Heiress Millicent Rogers in 1924, he was so broke that she had to buy the wedding ring. Last week, still broke and now divorced, he filed a petition in New York Supreme Court to have their 14-year-old son, Peter Salm, support him ($20,000 a year for himself, $10,000 a year for the expense of having his son visit, $35,000 for counsel fees). Reason: "It is the duty of a child possessing wealth to support a parent without funds." The Count did not win the lawsuit.

[23] *Evening Standard Journal*, Lincoln, NE, November 4, 1938

[24] Personal communication, Arturo Peralta-Ramos II

[25] Owens, Mitchell, "Fashion of the Times," *New York Times Magazine*, part 2, Fall 2001

[26] Hurst, Tricia, "Heiress Brings Lavish Lifestyle to Taos," *New Mexico Magazine*, November 1989

[27] Op. cit., Annette Tapert: 68

[28] Rogers, Millicent, A Letter from Millicent Rogers to John Joseph, August 1947, edited by Paul Peralta-Ramos, a participant in the events, Millicent Rogers Museum archives

[29] Personal communication, Arturo Peralta-Ramos II

[30] U.S. National Gallery of Art, *Contemporary American Indian Painting*, Smithsonian Institution, 1953

[31] Personal communication, Arturo Peralta-Ramos II

[32] Ibid.

[33] Austrian and skiing information, personal communication, David Cooper. Arturo II remembers his mother hiding a teen in her attic in St. Anton. He thought it may have been Kurt Jr.; however Kurt Jr. says it wasn't him.

[34] Ibid.

[35] Excerpt from a letter by Arturo H. Peralta-Ramos III, on December 20, 1984, seeking funds for a John Joseph Memorial Library at the Millicent Rogers Museum

[36] Personal communication, Arturo Peralta-Ramos II

37 Schuschnigg, Kurt von; Janet von Schuschnigg (2012-03-09).
   When Hitler Took Austria (Kindle Locations 1485-1492).
   Ignatius Press. Kindle Edition.

38 Op. cit., Mitchell Owens

39 Personal communication, Arturo Peralta-Ramos II

40 Op. cit., Annette Tappert: 60

41 Op. cit. Tricia Hurst

42 Personal communication, Arturo Peralta-Ramos II

43 "From Quarter-Deck to Cooking Pot" essay by Michael D Coe and
   Ernesto Vitetti, from the *The Wilder Shores of Gastronomy*, Ed. Alan
   Davison with Helen Saberi, Ten Speed Press, 2002. (Note: the author
   is incorrect in that the Millicent Rogers Museum is a Southwest
   Museum and was founded by her sons Arturo and Paul Peralta-Ramos
   in 1956 after her death)

44 *Observer*, 10 May 1959: 19

45 Museum of Modern Art, New York, press release January 1949,
   a performance of FAÇADE by (Dame) Edith Sitwll and music by
   William Walton. All spelling and punctuation are Millicent Rogers.
   The Sitwells refer to Dame Edith and her brother Osbert Sitwell.

Chapter 4 – War Years

46 Owens, Mitchell, *New York Times*, "Desert Flower", August 19, 2001

47 *Washington Post*, May 27, 1940

48 Personal communication with Gordon Calhoun, Editor/Historian,
   Hampton Roads Naval Museum, referring to the book, *Claremont
   Manor: a History* by Eve S. Gregory

49 Hoopes, Townsend, *Driven Patriot*, Knopf, NY, 1992: 218

50 Op. cit., Annette Tappert

51 Nathan, Jean, "To the Manor Born," *Vogue Living Issue*: 76

52 Op. cit., Gordon Calhoun

53 Millicent's letters courtesy of the Harry Ransom Humanities Research
   Center, The University of Texas at Austin

54 Gregory, Eve S., *Claremont Manor: a History*, Plummer Printing Co.,
   Inc. Petersburg, VA, 1990: 86

55 Personal communication, Arturo Peralta-Ramos II

56 Op. cit., Gregory, Eve S.: 86

57 *The Richmond News Leader*, Thursday, November 12, 1942

58 Conant, Jennet, *The Irregulars: Roald Dahl and the British Spy Ring in
   Wartime Washington*, Simon and Schuster, 2009

[59] Personal communication, David Cooper, who cites Arturo II and Fairlie, Gerard, *Flight Without Wings: The Biography Of Hannes Schneider*, Hodder and Stoughton, London, 1957

[60] Op. cit., Adam Lewis: 137

[61] Op. cit., Adam Lewis:154

[62] Personal communication, Arturo Peralta-Ramos II

[63] Roald Dahl Google Timeline: http://www.google.com/search?q= Roald+Dahl&ie=utf-8&oe=utf-8&aq=t&rls=org.mozilla:en-US: official&client=firefox-a#q=Roald+Dahl&hl=en&client=firefox-a&hs =Evc&rls=org.mozilla:en-US:official&prmd=ivnsbo&tbs=tl:1&tbo=u& ei=pFsoTpRSiNOIAq_OpLAC&sa=X&oi=timeline_result&ct=title&res num=22&ved=0CKIBEOcCMBU&bav=on.2,or.r_gc.r_pw.&fp=44eb8 ccc40613db6&biw=1067&bih=718

[64] Op. cit., Conant

[65] *New York Times*, book review of *The Irregulars*, October 19, 2008

[66] Stephenson, William, *Man Called Intrepid*, Ballantine, 1979: 184-185

[67] Op. cit., Jennet Conant: 120 – 21

[68] Ibid.: 112

[69] Ibid.: 113

[70] Ibid.: 270

[71] Personal communication, Arturo Peralta-Ramos II

[72] Op. cit., Jennet Conant: 113 - 114

[73] Ibid.: 271

[74] This interesting introduction is from Wikipedia and is not verified.

[75] Personal communication, Arturo Peralta-Ramos II

[76] Op. cit., Annette Tappert: 64

[77] Lycett, Andrew, Ian Fleming, *The Man Behind James Bond*, Turner Publications, 1996: 167

[78] Ibid.: 32 and 333

[79] Vreeland, Diana, *D.V.*, Knopf, 1984: 142

[80] Ibid.: 121

Chapter 5 – Hollywood

[81] Stefko, Jill, "Valentino's Ghost and Cursed Ring," http://ghosts-hauntings.suite101.com/article.cfm/valentinos_ghost_ haunts_estate, July 26, 2007

[82] Wallace, David, "Signature in Silver," *Fashion*, Friday, May 17, 1991: E10

[83] Personal communication, Arturo Peralta-Ramos II

[84] Ibid.

[85] Ibid.

[86] Ibid.

[87] Ibid.

[88] Ibid.

[89] Tornabene, Lyn, *Long Live the King, a Biography of Clark Gable,* G.P. Putnam's Sons, 1976, pg. 334

[90] Personal Communication, Arturo Peralta-Ramos II

[91] Furniss, Harry, *Family & Friends: Memoirs Three*, Trafford Publishing, March 2003, pg. 142

[92] Faulkner Trivia site: http://www.mcsr.olemiss.edu/~egjbp/faulkner/trivia.html#hol4

[93] Personal communication, Arturo Peralta-Ramos II

Chapter 6 – "The Mountain Held Me in Taos"

[94] The traditional spelling of Tony's surname is Lujan. Mabel Dodge changed the spelling to Luhan so that her Anglo friends could pronounce it with ease.

[95] Personal communication, Arturo Peralta-Ramos II.

All of this chapter, including Millicent's words in italics, were from Arturo's written memories to the authors.

Chapter 7 – Life in Taos

[96] Hurst, Tricia, "Heiress Brings Lavish Lifestyle to Taos," *New Mexico Magazine*, November 1989

[97] Boudica (pronounced /'bu : dika/; also spelled Boudicca), formerly known as Boadicea (/bou.ædi'si : a/) and known in Welsh as "Buddug") (d. AD 60 or 61) was a queen of the Brittonic Iceni tribe of what is now known as East Anglia in England, who led an uprising of the tribes against the occupying forces of the Roman Empire.

[98] Op. cit., Millicent Rogers' letters to John Joseph, Millicent Rogers Museum archives

[99] Recollections by John Joseph, Millicent Rogers Museum archives

[100] *Fashion and Identity*, Millicent Rogers Museum Publication, Taos, 2004

[101] Brett, Dorothy, "Millicent Rogers in Taos," undated manuscript, The Dorothy Brett/John Manchester collection, Center for Southwest Studies, University of New Mexico, Albuquerque

[102] Personal communication, Carmen Velarde

[103] Personal communication, Arturo Peralta-Ramos II

[104] Op. cit., Dorothy Brett

[105] Personal communication, Arturo Peralta-Ramos II

[106] Ibid.

[107] Ibid.

[108] Millicent Rogers Museum archives

[109] Ibid.

[110] Personal communication, Patricia Concha Murphy

[111] Op. cit., Brett, Dorothy

[112] Tedlock, Jr., E.W., *Frieda Lawrence, the Memoirs and Correspondence*, Octagon Press, Ltd., 1982, pg. 11

[113] Rudnick, Lois, *Mabel Dodge Luhan, New Woman, New Worlds*, University of New Mexico Press, Albuquerque, 1987: 328

[114] Personal communication, Miranda Levy

[115] Op. cit., Harry Ransom Humanities Research Center

[116] Op. cit., Hurst

[117] Op. cit., Henry Ransom

[118] Op. cit., Hurst

Chapter 8 - Final Resting Place

[119] Op. cit., Dorothy Brett

[120] *El Crepusculo*, Taos, Thursday, January 8, 1953

[121] Personal communication, Arturo Peralta-Ramos II

[122] Ibid.

[123] Op. cit., Dean Porter

[124] Op. cit., Millicent Rogers Museum

SELECTED BIBLIOGRAPHY

Archival Sources
Harry Ransom Humanities Research Center, The University of Texas at Austin
Center for Southwest Studies, University of New Mexico, Albuquerque, New Mexico
Millicent Library, Fairhaven, Massachusetts
Millicent Rogers Museum Archives, Taos, New Mexico
Southwest Research Center UNM-Taos, New Mexico

Periodicals
El Crepusculo, Taos, Thursday, January 8, 1953
Evening Standard Journal, Lincoln, NE, November 4, 1938
Fort Worth Star-Telegram, Fort Worth, 1920
Hurst, Tricia, "Heiress Brings Lavish Lifestyle to Taos," *New Mexico Magazine*, November 1989
Morris, Roger, *Architectural Digest*, "Millicent Rogers' New Mexico Legacy," Vol. 50, No. 6, June 1993
Nathan, Jean, "To the Manor Born," *Vogue Living Issue*
New York Evening Post, May 29, 1907
New York Times, book review of *The Irregulars*, October 19, 2008
Nordyke, Maryann Z., "Grand Inheritance," *Lapidary Journal*, March 1993: 34
Observer, 10 May 1959
Ogden Standard Examiner, Ogden, July 1921
Owens, Mitchell, "Fashion of the Times," *New York Times Magazine*, Fall 2001
Owens, Mitchell, *New York Times*, "Desert Flower", August 19, 2001
Washington Post, May 27, 1940
The Richmond News Leader, Thursday, November 12, 1942
Wallace, David, "Signature in Silver," *Fashion*, Friday, May 17, 1991: E10

Interviews: 2007-2010
David Cooper
Patricia Concha Murphy
Bill Green
Miranda Levy
Arturo Peralta-Ramos

Jackie Peralta-Ramos
Tony Reyna
Julian Robles
Mark Romero
Rosmarie Matt from Haus Rudi Matt in St. Anton, Austria
Wiltraud Salm
Peter Schaeffer
Kurt Von Schuschnigg, Jr.
Carmen Velarde
Lee Vigil

General Sources

Burke, Flannery, *From Greenwich Village to Taos, Primitivism and Place at Mabel Dodge Luhan's*, University Press of Kansas, 2008

Coe, Michael D. and Ernesto Vitetti, *The Wilder Shores of Gastronomy, "From Quarter-Deck to Cooking Pot,"* Ed. Alan Davison with Helen Saberi, Ten Speed Press, 2002

Conant, Jennet, *The Irregulars: Roald Dahl and the British Spy Ring in Wartime Washington*, Simon and Schuster, 2009

Davis, Paul K. *100 Decisive Battles: From Ancient Times to the Present,* Oxford University Press, 2001

Bernard Boutet de Monvel, catalogue, Barry Friedman Ltd., exhibition dates: November 1, 1994–January 7, 1995

Fairlie, Gerard, *Flight Without Wings: The Biography Of Hannes Schneider,* Hodder and Stoughton, 1957

Fashion and Identity, Millicent Rogers Museum, Taos, 2004

Fonda, Jane, *My Life So Far*, Random House, 2005

Furniss, Harry, *Family & Friends: Memoirs Three*, Trafford Publishing, March 2003

Gregory, Eve S., *Claremont Manor: a History*, Plummer Printing Co., Inc., Petersburg, VA, 1990

Hoopes, Townsend, *Driven Patriot*, Knopf, NY, 1992

Hyde, H. Montgomery, *Secret Intelligence Agent*, St. Martin's Press, 1983

Leary, Louis, ed. *Mark Twain's Letters to Mary*, Columbia University Press, 1961

Lewis, Adam, *Van Day Truex, The Man Who Defined Twentieth-Century Taste and Style*, Viking Studio, 2001

Lukacs, John, *Five Days in London, May 1940*, Yale University Press, 1999

Lycett, Andrew, Ian Fleming, *The Man Behind James Bond*, Turner Publications, 1996

MacTaggart, Ross, *The Golden Century: Classic Motor Yachts, 1830-1930*, W.W. Norton & Co., 2001

Messent, Peter, *Mark Twain and Male Friendship: The Twichell, Howells, and Rogers Friendships*, Oxford University Press, 2009

Porter, Dean A., et al, *Taos Artists and Their Patrons, 1898–1950*, Snite Museum of Art, May 1999, especially note the chapter "Three Women of Taos" by Elizabeth Cunningham.

Pratt, Fletcher, *The Battles That Changed History*, Dover Publications, 2000

Rudnick, Lois, *Mabel Dodge Luhan, New Woman, New Worlds*, University of New Mexico Press, Albuquerque, 1987

Stephenson, William, *Man Called Intrepid*, Ballantine, 1979

Stephenson, W.S., ed., *British Security Coordination: The Secret History of British Intelligence in the Americas 1940-1945*, Fromm International, 1998

Tapert, Annette and Edkins, Diana, *The Power of Style: The Women Who Defined the Art of Living Well*, Crown Press, 1994

Tedlock, Jr., E.W., *Frieda Lawrence, the Memoirs and Correspondence*, Octagon Press, Ltd., 1982

Tisdale, Shelby J, *Fine Indian Jewelry of the Southwest: The Millicent Rogers Museum Collection*, Museum of New Mexico Press, 2006

Tornabene, Lyn, *Long Live the King, a Biography of Clark Gable*, G.P. Putnam's Sons, 1976

U.S. National Gallery of Art, *Contemporary American Indian Painting*, Smithsonian Institution, 1953

Schuschnigg, Kurt von; Janet von Schuschnigg (2012-03-09), *When Hitler Took Austria* (Kindle Locations 1485-1492), Ignatius Press, Kindle Edition.

Vreeland, Diana, *D.V.*, Knopf, 1984

Waters, Frank, *Of Time and Change*, Mac Murry and Beck, Denver, 1998

Internet Sources

Faulkner Trivia site:
http://www.mcsr.olemiss.edu/~egjbp/faulkner/trivia.html#hol4

Stefko, Jill, "Valentino's Ghost and Cursed Ring," July 26, 2007 http:// ghosts-hauntings.suite101.com/article.cfm/valentinos_ghost_haunts_ estate

Roald Dahl Google Timeline:
http://www.google.com/search?q=Roald+Dahl&ie=utf-8&oe=utf-8&aq=t&rls=org.mozilla:en-US:official&client=firefox-a#q=Roal

d+Dahl&hl=en&client=firefox-a&hs=Evc&rls=org.mozilla:en-US
:official&prmd=ivnsbo&tbs=tl:1&tbo=u&ei=pFsoTpRSiNOIAq_
OpLAC&sa=X&oi=timeline_result&ct=title&resnum=22&ved=0CKIBE
OcCMBU&bav=on.2,or.r_gc.r_pw.&fp=44eb8ccc40613db6&biw=1067&
bih=718

CPSIA information can be obtained at www.ICGtesting.com
Printed in the USA
BVOW11*0321070814

361859BV00002B/2/P

9 780983 871279